THE PURPOSE ROADMAP.

Clarify your purpose. Define your calling.
Claim the fulfilling life you're meant to have.

MICK LOLEKONDA

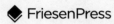 FriesenPress

Suite 300 - 990 Fort St
Victoria, BC, V8V 3K2
Canada

www.friesenpress.com

ISBN
978-1-4602-9385-0 (Hardcover)
978-1-4602-9386-7 (Paperback)
978-1-4602-9387-4 (eBook)

1. SELF-HELP, PERSONAL GROWTH, SUCCESS

Distributed to the trade by The Ingram Book Company

TABLE OF CONTENTS

For my parents, Omana Omoy Anyeke Brigitte and Okuka Lundja,
without whom I wouldn't be the person that I am today.

And for my sisters, Flore, Aurelie, Alison, and Victoria, the most fun,
loving, and strongest women I'm proud to know.

PREFACE

Before we get into this book, I'd like you to answer this question:

What does fulfillment look like to you?

Some of us want to have a fulfilling life but sometimes forget to visit or revisit this question in order to set or re-adjust the course of our lives. Set or re-adjust it so we experience, on a daily basis, the fact that we're making decisions we're satisfied with and, as a result, that we're moving in the right direction when it comes to creating as well as enjoying a fulfilling life.

So as we dive into this book, I encourage you to keep that in the back of your mind. What does fulfillment look like to you (and how does it look right now)?

Who is this book for?

If overnight results are what you're after, this book is not for you—you'll just feel that this book was a waste of time.

But if you embrace the idea that, for us to get the things that matter in life, it unfortunately takes time and requires us to go through a process (of transformation), then this book is for you.

This is for you because its simple yet profound principles are meant to help you get a clearer sense of direction in life, work, and business.

I wrote this book for the person who—as I did at a critical time in my life—is clarifying their purpose and discerning what they're meant to do and for whom staying aligned to their purpose is an ongoing deep-rooted desire.

If this is you, I'm so happy that we found each other today. I can tell you that the journey ahead is an exciting one. Know that you're exactly where you need to be right now. Simply embrace where you find yourself in life today regardless of what you might be going through. Regardless, because it's about you having a unique and personal journey.

The past is now behind you, and the next chapter of your life—one that's filled with clear meaning and purpose—starts right now. So be grateful and honour it.

A little about myself

After getting my dual Bachelor of Science degree in Business Management and Computer Information Systems from Vermont's College of St. Joseph in 2003, I remember trying to rely on myself and my limited strength and intelligence to build my life and create success on my own. I wanted to feel that I was responsible for my own results and take all the credit for it—I did not believe that I needed a higher power to do that.

I can tell you that it left me feeling emotionally and spiritually depleted. It got me *nowhere*, a place where everything I felt I had worked so hard to build came crumbling down, about ten years later. More on that in the upcoming chapters.

That was the price I feel I had to pay for wanting to control my life.

After realizing how unsustainable and inefficient this approach was—losing everything you worked hard to achieve will certainly open your eyes—I reached a point where a life assessment and the need to do have a different life-building approach become alarmingly apparent.

If you find yourself in similar shoes and are now open to trying something different, you should know that you've come to the right place. You were *meant* to read this book.

A quick heads up

I'll be sharing, in this book, what I've learned and experienced first-hand in the thirteen years of what I call the purpose journey. My ideas and perspectives reflect a holistic approach to creating a fulfilling life. This will include addressing the topic of spirituality and God; however, don't be put off or frightened away. Belief in God *per se* is not required—only an acknowledgment of some sort of higher power, even if it's as amorphous as *the universe*.

You'll see me use the word God, Life, the One, interchangeably to keep things simple. You can think in terms of whatever you're comfortable with. At the end of the day, I believe that labels don't matter.

Since we're on the topic of spirituality, my intention is to address this topic from a universal perspective using universal topics and principles accessible to all, regardless of religious background.

My approach to spirituality is non-religious in nature though for me it *is* God-centered. You'll have to chance to see what led me to adopt this approach in this book as well. For now, know that this entire book is the result of a *spiritual* experiment I started back in the fall of 2012.

Everything I'll be sharing with you is the result of first-hand experience.

Why did I write this book?

This book is meant to give you an overview of both practical and spiritual principles that can help you—as it did me—clarify your purpose, calling, and mission in life. Whatever that looks like to you.

It is also meant to be a reference guide that you can refer to at any stage of your life.

I'm going to share with you practical steps that will support you in better navigating the purpose journey and its unique challenges while living life more intentionally.

This more intentional way of living is the type of life we choose to lead. One where we're aware of what it is that we want out of life, have the desire to know where we're going, learn what it takes to get there, and implement our newly acquired and assimilated knowledge for the benefit of living the best life we can—the best life we can, not only for ourselves, but for others as well. This is how I define living life intentionally.

It's important to recognize that *when we choose to live intentionally, by default, the life we lead becomes purposeful in nature.*

As someone who's intentionally lived the purpose journey for over a decade now, what I can share with you is this:

Once we start living our lives intentionally, we can expect challenges specific to this journey. Challenges that will impact us personally, spiritually, and career-wise and will affect our relationships, particularly our intimate ones.

This book will give you an overview of what's ahead and what to expect from it.

It is also designed to be a quick reference-guide so you can revisit fundamental concepts related to the purpose journey at any stage of your journey and life.

As you go through this book, you may find that some concepts resonate with you more than others. This is normal. As we grow, it's only natural that different concepts resonate with us at different stages of life.

My purpose journey (the context)

My purpose journey started in 2001 during a four-year stint in Vermont's College of St. Joseph as a French-speaking Congolese international student.

One day I was chilling in my dorm room before my next class, and the TV was tuned to the *Jerry Springer Show*. My virgin ears and eyes couldn't *believe* the content of the show—especially as a new-comer in the US. Talk about a culture shock! Not to say that the show particularly triggered what was about to happen next, but I suddenly felt that I wanted to know what my purpose in life was and what it was that I was meant to do. I wanted to know it so badly that, at times, it hurt and grew into a consuming fire.

Later that same year I was again chilling in my room except this time Oprah was playing in the background. My attention suddenly got drawn to the guest she had on that day. As I kept on listening, Oprah asked her guest exactly what her occupation as a life coach was; at the time, not a lot of people knew what that was. As her guest explained herself, I'll never forget how suddenly overwhelmed I was with the deep resonance I felt to what she was saying.

I suddenly knew what I wanted to do in life: *I want to help people reach their goals while staying aligned with their purpose!*

This clear insight came from within in a way that was unmistakably crystal-clear and exciting, and from that point on, this feeling became my life-engine, my drive, and almost an obsession.

This drive led me on an exciting, fantastic—and sometimes frustrating—journey complete with its ups, downs, and sets of unique challenges.

I remember also thinking during those college days how cool it'd be to also earn a full-time income doing what I loved—that sounded like freedom to me. As an international student, the American Dream had gotten a hold of me.

I'm very clear today about what my purpose and calling in life are and how I'm meant to make a difference in people's lives, and in fact, nothing has changed since day one in terms of ensuring everything I do keeps me aligned with my purpose. I always made sure that every choice I made was one that I felt would get me closer to the answers I sought.

Because of everything I've learned on this purpose journey, I now feel very privileged to be in a position where I can simply share with you the practical things I've learned—and *continue* to learn—along the way including what is helpful and not so helpful.

I had no roadmap when I embarked on this unique journey, but you'll have one thanks to the content of this book and other resources available in the resources section. This way, you won't need to spend unnecessary extra time trying to figure things out through trial-and-error, as I did. Use my setbacks and insights as sign-posts. Know what to avoid and what to focus on and you'll enjoy a smoother ride than I did.

I want to get you where you envision yourself being. I want to help you efficiently navigate the road ahead—the highway of your purpose journey.

So let's get started.

With deep appreciation,
Mick.

"The unexamined life is not worth living."

—Socrates

1. UNDERSTANDING PURPOSE AND CALLING

Based on experience, I see *purpose* as the idea that drives us to:

- Grow because of our embedded desire to have a life that has meaning and a clear sense of direction.

- Want to know who we are at our very core.

- Realize how we fit into this world.

- Realize that life is not just about us (unless we choose to make it so) but about how we connect with others.

- Be in a position where we can help and serve others and/or our environment.

- Realize that there is more to life than living on auto-pilot (the alternative being to live life intentionally).

What's worth noticing about the idea of *purpose* is that it drives us to be increasingly aware of how we live our lives on a daily basis and, ultimately, get to a point where we find ourselves doing—and focusing on—the things that matter and fulfill us along the way. Regardless of the challenges we'll face, we can then be in a position to look back at our lives and feel satisfied.

This is one of the ways that the purpose journey is meant to impact us.

The difference between Purpose and Calling

We can get all sorts of answers around this question, which is fine. I'm here to share ideas in order to simplify this purpose equation so our minds can better wrap itself around the concept.

Earlier on in my purpose journey, the concept of *calling* was not even on my radar. I felt that once I'd define my purpose, that would be that, and I'd be satisfied. But it wasn't the case.

In my mind, *purpose* and *calling* were one and the same.

What ended up happening, however, was this. I realize what I wanted to do in life and thought, *Wow, this is my purpose!*

I then remember thinking, *Okay, now what?*

This happened because I didn't realize that there was a distinction between purpose and calling. Let me explain.

I see *purpose* as the one thing we're put on this earth to do while *why* as the reason for wanting to live that purpose. An example of this would be: To find a cure for cancer. That's a purpose in life. The why would for someone to say: "Because (fill in the blanks)."

As it helps with making the process of clarifying our purpose easier, I feel that it's important that we make the distinction between *purpose* and *why* since I see them being used interchangeably, when they have two distinct meanings based on their etymology. Purpose relates to intention, aim, goal, and comes from the Old French *porpos*, and proposer which is from the

Latin *pro* and the Old French *poser*: Put together, they mean to "put forth".

Why, as noun, relates to reason for action, grounds for action, motive, and the reason for something taking place. It comes from the Old French *cause* and directly from the Latin *causa*.

A *calling* (some use the word vocation), is the physical expression of the defined purpose. Using the example mentioned above, one's calling could be that of a researcher, a lab technician, a scientist. In other words, the *calling* is the vehicle by which one is able to make a unique contribution based on their combination of core strengths, natural abilities, experience, and ways of seeing the world, in order to realize their purpose.

In other words, you chase down your *purpose* in the vehicle of your *calling*.

I didn't make this distinction at first. That's why, when I finally knew that my purpose was to help people achieve their goals while staying aligned with their purpose, I found myself in place wondering how would I now go about living it out. This is when the search for my calling (or vocation) started.

I now had to figure out how to integrate my ideas, interests, passion, and core strengths into a meaningful occupation—the one that would best express what I was meant to do.

I had to figure out how my *purpose* would translate into a physical activity so to speak. This is where the idea of a calling or a vocation comes in.

Once we make this distinction, our search process for clear direction and answers streamlines. This streamlining then makes it easier for us to see where we find ourselves on this journey of self-discovery. We then know where to focus our energy, whether it'd be in clarifying our purpose or calling in life.

I've found from experience that, when someone is on this specific journey—whether it'd be a friend, a client, or a stranger that I'm supporting—adopting this perspective removes the unnecessary frustrations that result from a mind having a hard time focusing on one or the other (purpose or calling).

When the mind knows it needs to first focus on determining *purpose*, it'll do just that and put the question of *calling* on the back-burner, and vice-versa. It's a simple two-step process.

Defining Purpose and Calling

Clarifying our purpose and calling is a two-step process. It's a process that, however, doesn't need to be linear. What I mean is that we don't need to define our purpose first and then define our calling.

One could already have their calling (vocation), unbeknownst to them, but not realize how their occupation fits in the grand scheme of things. Their work, in this case, has no context in their mind. In other words, they don't know what their purpose is.

At this point they may not know the bigger reason for what it is that they're doing, which may impact their level of performance, engagement, and overall fulfillment.

In this scenario, it may be a good idea for them to start their search relative to clarifying their purpose, which, once determined, will help put their calling into a greater context. One where the individual can start to grasp the magnitude of their contribution and realize their own value.

That's why I mentioned earlier that the process to clarify purpose and calling is a two-step process that doesn't need to necessarily start with the definition of purpose. As long as your search for answers encompasses these two elements, you are on the right track.

People can fall into two categories:

1. They're led to figure out their purpose first because it'll make it easier for them to realize what their calling is or

2. They're already living out their purpose through their calling or vocation, but now need to put their calling into the context of their purpose so what they do now makes sense. Of course, in some cases, once they realize what their purpose is, finding a better suited vocation that is the physical expression of that purpose is necessary.

So which category do *you* fall into?

Real Life Mechanics
Signpost 1

"Your purpose in life is to find your purpose and give your whole heart and soul to it."

—Gautama Buddha

Finding and being able to articulate our purpose in life starts by having those guiding questions brought to the forefront of our mind so they can drive us towards the answers we seek. Without worrying about having to answer those now, the following life course-setting questions are to be kept in mind and revisited at any stage of life:

- What is my purpose in life? If I know what it is, can I articulate it?

- What is my calling in life in relation to my purpose? Is my *current* occupation an expression of my purpose?

- Do my purpose and calling align?

It is important to think of calling in relation to purpose because the ultimate goal is to have a vocational calling that ties back to our purpose. Often, people have occupations that are not connected to their purpose, which leads them to feel unfulfilled.

Regardless of whether you have clear answers to these questions, keep them tucked away in the back of your mind, for they will fast-track your ability to get to pursue the answers you seek. These questions set your life's course, so keep them in mind.

"He who has a why to live for can bear almost any how."

—Friedrich Nietzsche

Why is there need to know our purpose?

Not everyone wants or cares to know what their purpose in life is, and that's fine.

Whether you're curious to explore this concept or feel that you are driven by your purpose (defined or not yet defined), what follows are a few thoughts as to why it's important for us to know our purpose.

What I've noticed, based on my experience, is that when we become clear on what our purpose is, it not only puts everything we do in our lives into context, but it also helps bring the different areas of our lives together to work as a cohesive unit.

Knowing our purpose helps the different aspects of our lives to work as a cohesive unit within a defined context.

Those different pieces being relationships, career, spiritual growth, personal growth, health, and ability to serve others. And when those different pieces work cohesively, this is when our lives run on all cylinders and we get to experience a truly fulfilling life—one that is, at its core, driven by the spirit of service.

Some of us may not necessarily use the term spirit of service, but we all know what it means to want to help others or to want to make a difference.

If this is you, you're on the right track because being led by the spirit of service is a great indication that not only are you *meant* to do something greater and meaningful with your life but that you have a greater purpose worth clarifying.

As I intentionally embarked on this journey to define my purpose and calling in life, the experiences I had to go through helped me clarify *how* I was meant to help others and *who* I was meant to help and offer the most value to, in a way that was most impactful based on my core strengths and unique perspectives.

Knowing our purpose enables us to realize our unique true value in this world and to others. It speaks to what we've been called to do.

I feel that Oprah Winfrey summed it up well when she said:

"I believe there's a calling for all of us. I know that every human being has value and purpose. The real work of our lives is to become aware. And awakened. To answer the call."

How we fit in this world

Until we know how we fit into this world, our hearts will keep on searching for answers and direction. As long as we haven't giving up on successfully completing the search, there's still hope. Hope that our heart can find peace. Otherwise giving up is what I suggest *not* doing because we'll otherwise feel that something is missing, which in turn leads to feeling unfulfilled.

Why do you think we catch ourselves feeling a void and start looking externally—and to no avail—for what we think will fill that void, from jobs to relationships to thrills? And why, when they *seem* to fill our void, do they only do so temporarily?

It is because our deepest longing to know our unique function in this world goes unanswered. Our questions go unanswered initially because we don't know where to look, which leads us to knock on the wrong doors so-to-speak and pursue the wrong opportunities.

We take the wrong jobs. We get into the wrong relationships. We look into temporary fixes ranging from drugs, excessive partying, and thrill-seeking activities that unfortunately delay and prevent our ability to face the *important* questions within us:

- What do I really want to do with my life?

- Why am I delaying this?

- Is what I'm currently doing really what I want to do, or am I just going through the motion?

- What am I waiting for?

- Am I playing it safe?

- Why am I not taking a chance and going for it?

- What is the next step that will get me closer to living the life I desire to have?

- What is it that I need so I can transition into the life, (business) career I want?

- What does having a fulfilling life look like to me?

Only when we figure out to address our deepest longing, will our heart finds peace and the ability to settle.

Once our heart settles and our purpose—as well as our calling—has been defined, the next stage becomes focusing on honing the skills that will best equip us to carry out our unique task or mission. Our task requires our unique combination of skills, knowledge, and life experience.

At this stage, we start the process of building our legacy and life's work. It can come in the form of a specialty—the one thing that we'll be known for because only we can deliver the way can. What naturally follows is a specific type of life training experience or professional development opportunity that one must leverage in order to be the best at what they do.

Knowing our purpose also makes it easier for us to determine who and what is a natural fit in our now well-defined, purpose-driven life.

When we seek to fit in to the chaotic world that we know—with all its expectations—knowing our purpose gives us the ability to design our external and visible world as a reflection of our newly-defined and purpose-driven inner-world. Another way of saying this is designing the life we want in such a way that it resonates with and reflects what we know we deserve to have and are worthy of.

When we do this, the world around us starts reacting to us as opposed to us reacting to it.

Let the world react to you because the vision you have is what this broken world desperately needs—a place of refuge so it can heal and be better.

Life Pruning & Decluttering

When you prune a tree, shrub, or bush by cutting away dead or overgrown branches or stems, you increase fruitfulness and growth. When we apply this same process to our lives, we can also increase how rich and fulfilling our lives can be.

When we have a clearly defined purpose and the desire to live a fulfilled life, it becomes easier to declutter our lives, divesting ourselves of the things and relationships that add no value into our lives. *Life is about growth, and as such, we should only include what contributes to that.*

It's necessary to remove what doesn't fuel the richness, the sense of growth, and the sense of fulfillment in our lives. At this point, it's about learning to make the right key decisions and being comfortable saying no to what doesn't serve our meaningful purpose. Choosing not to settle is key.

Whether we're talking about opportunities or people, life is about quality rather than quantity. It is about living in a way that both aligns and resonates with our purpose—who we are at our core.

Simply put, people either add to our lives or they take away from it; the same goes for opportunities, jobs, businesses.

Things either add value or they don't.

What becomes necessary, therefore, is for us to define what adding value into our lives means. After we are clear on what adding value means to us, viewing everything in our lives through the lens of that definition should make it easier to know who or what to keep in our lives and who or what to let go of.

Keep revisiting your definitions. See how they have served you. Check to see if perhaps they have evolved and, if so, how your life now aligns with them. *Keep what serves you and your life, and have the strength and courage to let go of the rest.*

Unmatched Focus

Another benefit of knowing our purpose is the unmatched level of focus that having a defined purpose brings into our lives. A defined purpose leads us to focus on things and people that matter, which in turn, leads to a decluttered life.

When done right, a decluttered life then leads to a life filled with peace, joy, and fulfillment—and devoid of unnecessary stress.

When a defined purpose and unmatched focus go hand-in-hand, one can expect to get where they envision being more efficiently and enjoy life more because their load is much lighter.

Time

Knowing our purpose also helps to protect our most precious commodity: Time.

Time is not wasted when we clearly know our purpose because we then only focus on the things that matter and align with our purpose-driven life.

From the people we attract and choose to develop relationships with, to opportunities we should to capitalize on, to the choices we can now make that support our core values and aspirations, to what we now have the courage to say no to, the value of our time becomes more evident. And when we value our time more highly we better utilize the time we have.

Making the best use of our time and efficiently living life is the result of the choices we make. It becomes about what we intentionally and consciously say yes and no to and what we choose to focus on, namely, the few things—if not the one thing—that bring us the most fulfillment, peace, and joy.

This purpose-driven life becomes more about doing the few things and being with the few people that matter most and bring us fulfillment and vice-versa. Instead of filling up our calendar and stretching ourselves thin trying to satisfy everyone, this renewed focus is what leads to truly enjoying life with an increased sense of freedom.

Doesn't this sound like a much better way of living?

It's about the bigger picture and the desired outcome for our lives. It's about creating the needed space so we feel that we're running our lives—as opposed to our lives running us—thanks to the choices we make in regards to the people and opportunities that we allow to enter our lives and stay for as long as they need to be there.

Peace

Another benefit of knowing our purpose is the peace that this knowing brings into our lives. *There's a certain peace that settles once we know our direction in life and where we're headed.*

Realizing how we fit into this world and what our unique contribution is satisfies the deepest longing of our heart. It is the longing of having meaning and direction in our lives, which fuels our sense of fulfillment and emotional stability in our lives despite the curve balls that life can throw at us.

As I came across this quote, I thought that Edgar Lee Masters put it beautifully:

> *To put meaning in one's life may end in madness,*
> *But life without meaning is the torture*
> *Of restlessness and vague desire—*
> *It is a boat longing for the sea and yet afraid.*

Core Values

Being clear on what our purpose is deepens the connection we have to our core values and our understanding of them. This, in turn, makes it easier to live *authentically*, which is to say *in a way that feels true to our-selves.*

I define core values as the concepts entrenched in our hearts that help dictate how we choose to be engaged with the world around us and how we choose to connect to other human-beings. They also affect what actions we choose to live by—and who we choose to associate with—in order to reflect those core values. The exciting challenge is to be crystal-clear about what our core values are so that we can then live a life in a way where we simply *are* and offer ourselves to the world as we *are*—in other words, in a way that's authentic.

Those core values can include integrity, service, adventure, honesty, health, freedom, love, personal growth, faith... the list goes on.

Most people don't know themselves intimately, myself included.

Some do so more than others. When it comes to me, this purpose journey and its spiritual dimension has helped me go deeper within myself and be so much clearer about what my core values are.

Knowing our core values is the type of awareness that we must have because it's through this knowledge that we add true value to those around us and the causes we hold close to our hearts. Not only that but it also makes it easier for us to realize who we can offer the most value to.

If you feel driven to live a fulfilling life, help people and make a difference; being in touch with your core values and knowing what they are is key. What are your core values as they apply to all areas of your life?

It is also key because, as we strive to have and maintain a fulfilling life, we must remember that fulfillment is created when the choices we make, the people we choose to associate with, the relationships we choose to nurture, and the opportunities we pursue must speak to our core values. When those don't align, feeling unfulfilled is the natural consequence of the misalignment.

The clearer you are regarding what your core values are, the easier it'll be to attract, recognize, and keep the opportunities and people who resonate with you the most at this point of your life. People who you are ultimately called to lead, support, help, care for, love, and serve.

Freedom

We're constantly bombarded by external expectations ranging from family, culture, and the media. Directly or indirectly, we are told how to look; how to be behave; what's cool versus what's not; what the standard of beauty is; what we should have; what we should do with our lives; and of course, what kind of romantic love we should aspire to have. In short, we're conditioned to feel that we're not enough, that we'll never have enough, and that there is a need to be perfect in every way. Most importantly, we are conditioned to feel entitled to all of this.

The impact of this never-enough culture was well researched by Brené Brown in her book *Daring Greatly* where what she highlighted put into words what I was thinking. She referred to the cultural environment we live in as one that cultivates the shame-based fear of being ordinary. "The fear of never feeling extraordinary enough to be noticed, to be loveable, to belong, or to cultivate a sense of purpose."

Those external expectations, if we're not careful, eat away at our ability to speak and live our truth. *By taking the steps to clarify our purpose and live it out, we get to boldly reclaim who we are and stop reacting to the world around us.*

Instead, we become a proactive participant, an initiator, a creator, a change-maker in this world. A world that now starts reacting to us because our stand and action become counter-cultural.

Through this process, we end up breaking the emotional and spiritual chains that have bound us—chains that prevented us from fully expressing ourselves in a way that's authentic, chains that kept our spirit from blossoming and kept us from recognizing our unique contributing value to this world.

I've found that when we have the courage to go deeper within ourselves—regardless of what we might find out about ourselves during the descent and how reluctant we can be to re-live negative emotions and experiences—this uncovers a path that can lead us to the emotional freedom that some of us don't even realize we're seeking. I speak from experience.

This ended up being the biggest realization I ultimately had regarding the point of this journey.

When I speak about emotional freedom, I speak about the type of inner-freedom that helps us better share, communicate, and act on our core values.

It's the kind of freedom that helps better assess opportunities and relationships that come our way because we're marching to the beat of our own drum.

Marching to the beat of our drum allows us to dictate what and how things happen in our lives in a way that best satisfies our inner-need for peace, contentment, joy, and fulfillment. That's true emotional freedom.

Once emotional freedom has been reached, we gain the ability to stand stronger against external social and cultural pressures that've been impacting us all along. Will those pressures still be there? Yes, absolutely. Such pressures are as relentless as gravity. The difference is that emotional freedom better equips us to recognize these pressures and deal with them accordingly thanks to how grounded we now are. The goal is not only to become grounded in our core values, but also spiritually grounded— something I'll show how to do in the later chapters chapters with a clarity tool that I refer to as the Peaceful State Process (PSP). Now that's liberating.

As a result of that freedom, we can now impact the world around us from the inside, from within us and radiating out and into the world. In other words, we've transitioned from reacting to the world around us to creating into it.

Real Life Mechanics
Signpost 2

When you have a definite purpose for your life, clarity comes faster, which leads to more conviction in your direction, which usually leads to faster decisions... the best decisions... the best experiences.

—Gary Keller with Jay Papasan, *The One Thing*

■ Determine in which areas of your life you can make the shift from reacting to creating.

■ Describe your desired lifestyle. Be honest with yourself, and don't allow your mind to play interference with doubts and fear. Let your heart speak. Let the voice of truth come out.

■ Don't worry about *how* you'll make your desired vision happen because this is not the point of the exercise. Think about where you are today and begin with your desired picture as the starting point.

"The single greatest difference between curious, growing people and those who aren't is the belief that they can learn, grow, and change."

—John C. Maxwell, *The 15 Invaluable Laws of Growth*

2. DISCOVERING YOUR PATH

No compromise

It takes an uncompromising, burning, and sometimes obsessive (I'm guilty of that) desire to know what our purpose is and how to live it out.

The more we obsess over it, the higher the chances we have of uncovering it and being able to articulate it.

This drive is what I like to call our life fuel. It leads us to experience all that we can so we can grow into the person we're meant to be for others and the world—that person being the full expression of core strengths, core values, passion, and our ability to make the greatest impact with our unique contribution. In other word, be the person we've been called to be.

Diving into the idea of life fuel, I refer to our purpose being just that because, like the fuel we use in our cars, it's the key element that enables our life engine to get going. It allows us to drive forward in life as opposed to staying in park. Without purpose, we compromise not only our ability to experience life to the fullest in a way that goes beyond what we could ever anticipate, but also our ability to see what we're truly capable in achieving in this lifetime.

Through this process, we are led to gather the clues that will help clarify our purpose, while gathering the necessary skills, knowledge, and experiences along the way that will allow us to perform our vocational calling at our best.

How committed are you to fully knowing and then articulating your purpose?

What does it mean to be committed in this context?

It means committing to:

- Being open to growth opportunities coming your way.

- Courageously letting go of opportunities and even relationships that have run their course.

- Be willing to take chances.

- Learning as much as you can from your current life circumstances and opportunities.

- Be willing to face your fear of rejection and failure and push past it.

- Commit to being resilient and bouncing back quickly from whatever setbacks you experience, as heartbreaking and crushing as they might be.

Never letting go of our dream

Some of us have that *one dream*, which can also be referred to as life vision.

The dream I'm talking about is the one that surfaced one day and simply felt *right*. Regardless of whether we've experienced it or not, that dream is the picture of the life we envision for ourselves. One that brings us fulfillment in every way.

In that dream, we see ourselves doing exactly what we want and we see how we want to do it. We also see who we're meant to impact in a meaningful way.

Regardless of whether we can remember, barely remember, or have forgotten our dream, answers related to defining our purpose are contained in that dream. Why? Because this dream comes out of our heart unfiltered and untainted in a way that ignites intoxicating emotions that feel *right* and make us realize how our lives should feel. It is exhilarating and uplifts our spirit. The details of the dream are significant, but just as important is our ability and willingness to (re)connect with the emotions it occasioned.

Those emotions are our life compass. They're the ones we must learn to rely on because they confirm whether we're headed in the right direction or not. Whether we getting closer/warmer to our desired experience or distancing ourselves from it and growing colder.

If you happen to have almost forgotten about your dream or life vision—the way I did back in 2012—find a way to remember what that dream was like. In my case, the beating life had given me (or I had allowed it to give me) led me to lose almost all hope. Ever felt that way?

This is what happens over time when things don't go our way. We start to live life on autopilot and allow life to run us—instead of living life intentionally and refusing to be denied of what is rightfully ours: fulfillment. Next thing you know, the unfortunate circumstances we go through—the roadblocks and setbacks—erode our dream little by little.

If this is you, don't give up! Revisit your dream or life vision and see if those same desired emotions are ignited today the same way they were when your dream first surfaced.

Don't worry about whether you can make that dream an immediate reality or not. The point is simply to be honest with yourself and ask:

If money, resources, and roadmap were not an issue, would I still want to make that dream or life vision, a reality?

If the answer is yes, then the next step is simply to find a way to make the dream reality. It's by doing so that we all find ourselves propelled forward in pursuit of ways to realize our purpose.

The answers will undeniably come. But only when we choose to take the one next step and make course-corrections along the way. This is how what we're meant to be doing gets revealed to us. We choose to take the next step, and the next step, and the next after that.

Our responsibility is to nurture and protect our dream or life vision at all cost by not allowing anyone or anything to extinguish it—including ourselves.

We unfortunately stand in our own way sometimes, especially with excuses. Find the strength to work past them and simply do what you need to do.

Curiosity

Being curious and relentless in our search for answers is another needed ingredient that can help us clarify our purpose.

By being curious, I mean being the type of person that allows themselves to see where a new opportunity or idea—sometimes new or foreign—will lead them without prematurely pulling the plug.

Curiosity is what keeps our mind and spirit open. Adopting this mindset allows us to walk uncharted territories by having faith in our guided footsteps, which can also be referred to as the faith walk.

Having faith is key because we can never exactly predict or imagine where we're headed, what we're meant to learn along the way, and how our impact on others will look.

The faith walk, when adopted, allows us to be guided towards the needed experiences and the right people so we end up better equipped to carry out our task and, as a result, fulfil our unique calling in life.

Coming back to the idea of being curious. Curiosity puts us in a better position to take risks. It sets us on the road less travelled, and we can be pleasantly surprised by what awaits us down this path. I can attest to that. I know I wouldn't, in a million years, have anticipated all the twists and turns I experience on this journey, or who I'd meet, or even that I'd be able to deliver this book to you today.

Curiosity helps us get traction towards the answers we seek. It also makes us less likely to dismiss opportunities and people that are sent our way to add onto our lives in some way, shape, or form.

So when an opportunity to grow, learn, or even to meet someone present itself, let's develop the habit of pursuing the opportunity and see where it'll lead. Strive to be curious, and it'll pay dividends. The question is where can you be more curious?

Think of areas of your life where it's easy for you to be dismissive instead of being open and see where you might be led?

For example, we meet someone for the first time and they invite us out for coffee, but for whatever reason we decline the invitation out of hand without knowing what could've happen had we gone to coffee with them.

Or someone says hello to us, and we either don't respond or cut the conversation short because of our preconceived ideas or prejudices at that particular moment. Here again, there's no way to know where that conversation could've led to.

Or someone is presenting an idea or concept that challenges our way of thinking, and rather than hearing them out, we simply dismiss what they are saying. Dismissing an argument instead of engaging in dialogue and means we miss the opportunity to exchange perspectives and see where such an exchange could lead.

Figuring out the *how,* the vehicle

The tricky thing about pursuing the idea of purpose—which feels so abstract—is finding a way to make it a tangible thing so we can actually define it and live it out. This is where the idea of calling (or vocation) comes in. As mentioned earlier in this book, I like to look at calling as the concrete expression of the defined purpose.

If we are to use the example of *helping find a cure for cancer* as being someone's purpose in life, then being a scientist, a lab technician, a volunteer, or someone fundraising for cancer research might be their calling. A calling that is directly related to their purpose is that purpose's concrete expression and a way to live out the said purpose.

The challenge becomes finding the right vehicle that can help us live out our purpose and stay aligned with it. One must determine which vehicle will help them live out their purpose.

A good way to determining if you have the right vehicle is to find and look at someone that has a particular business or job (especially someone who's been in it for over a decade). If you currently have a job, look at the person with the position your career path within the company could lead you to. Does it feel like this is where you *want* to end up ultimately? How about their lifestyle and the way they impact people? Does it resonate with you? If you can't seem to find someone who makes you think, *THIS is what I want to do! This is the kind of life I want to have!* then keep on searching around you and online.

The same process can be applied anytime you find that whatever you've been doing either doesn't fully inspire growth and excitement in you or no longer does in the way it used to.

Looking for the *how* externally

How to get there? What do I think will satisfy and fulfill me?

Those are the kind of questions that, if we're not careful, can lead us to go look for answers in the wrong places.

This search for purpose and calling is a challenge, and often people struggle, get frustrated, and end up feeling stuck and overwhelmed.

The big question becomes *how do I go about clarifying my purpose in order to define my vehicle?*

Beyond this question, we must also find the courage to let go of a vehicle that, deep down, we know is not the concrete expression of our purpose. Of course, if the current vehicle affords us time to *find* our calling as well as dedicate ourselves to it full-time if we so choose, then we must learn to be grateful for it until it's time to let go of it.

When that time comes, there's no shame in letting go of what's not working or isn't the right fit. Let go and look for something else. Look for the right vehicle whether it's through online research, or asking people around you, or simply trying on new opportunities you're drawn to. But only after being clear on what would be the ideal situation and lifestyle for you despite *not knowing* the precise make of the vehicle that will get you there. The important thing is to get the wheels in motion so that, as you move forward, answers regarding which vehicle to use become clearer. Trust the process and remain hopeful that your intentionality will drive you to the answers you seek sooner than later. For now, simply know that the dream you hold dear is reachable.

If you are not free from the expectations of other people or the attachment to the perceived status or your current role, you need to find the strength to let go of all that because this is what I call ego-based living. Ego-based living prevents us from living intentionally and authentically. When operating from an ego-based standpoint, we react to the world, our culture, and even our family in a way that leads us to passively adapt to the ways of the world around us, preventing us from speaking our truth and robbing us of our chance to influence the world. Our spirit, in the process, erodes. By having to satisfy various external demands and expectations, we ultimately become slaves to them; we become fragmented, which leads to the unnecessary tensions and frustrations associated with always having to perform and prove ourselves and are pulled in different directions at once.

The opposite of this is what I call self-based living. This is what I suggest striving for and a tool like the Peaceful State Process (PSP) can help with that. This way of life strengthens our spirit. It allows to reconnect on a deeper level with who we are at the core and what our values are. It allows us to continually build the inner-strength that we need in order to stand for what we believe in and live out those beliefs and core values.

Spiritually speaking, it's a place where we learn to live as one with life, with God. But what does this mean exactly?

It means being in a place where we simply live and go through life understanding how life works and how we need to show up in the world for ourselves and for others. It means being in a place where there is profound peace, fulfillment, love, and contribution in a way that speaks to us deeply. It means being in a place free of the emotional bondage that results from the way our culture, media, and relationships have disassociated us from our true selves. When operating from a self-based standpoint, we are whole and can present ourselves as whole to those around us and to the world. We need to become authentic, spiritually strong, and grounded. We need to be emotionally free, alive, and moving in one purposeful direction. The roadmap in this book will help you get there.

An important thing to keep in mind as you embark on this new chapter of your life is to know to cut your losses. When is the right to let go of an opportunity? It's unfortunately difficult to provide a straight answer to this question. We all have unique journeys that present us with unique experiences. The important thing is to walk the journey because *this* is ultimately what will help strengthen our sixth sense or guided intuition. And it is our sixth sense that helps us feel that our lives are about to move in a different direction and lets us know when we've outgrown our jobs, businesses, and relationships and it's time to move on.

But what I can say is that with experience and a more developed sixth sense—the Peaceful State Process (PSP) can help with that—one can learn to sense when things are coming to an end and it's time to transition out of there.

Finding a mentor or mentors

A mentor is someone who has the breadth of experience that, when you tap into it, allows you to get to your desired path faster and in the most efficient way possible. They have accomplished—or helped others accomplish—what you yourself seek to achieve in the long-run. In other words, they have the fruit on the tree and because of it are easy to emulate.

The first kind of mentors that we can have are those we get to work directly with. They are usually great to work with when we've pushed ourselves as far as can and have plateaued. It's a concept similar to an athlete whose performance has plateaued and needs a mentor or coach to get them to the next level. There are mentors for all sorts of budgets and needs using various platforms. From one-on-one mentorship—like the ones I offer—to group mentorships, even online mentorships, there are many options for you to choose from. Determine first the amount of personal attention you require and, from there, which option would best suit your current need while fitting within your budget.

We can also get access to various mentors through books, audios, podcasts, apps. These options are convenient, easy to take advantage of, and can help quick-start your learning and implementation journey.

Regardless of what kind of mentor you seek, first determine what is your end-career/business goal is. Then see who embodies it and offers to teach others to do the same. Search online and/or ask those around you for mentors they recommend and have worked with.

Looking for the right vehicle within, i.e., the *how*

The thing that never occurred to me in the early stages of my purpose journey was that I needed to look for answers *within*.

More specifically, I had to turn to a Higher Power for answers and direction.

Didn't see this one coming did you?

Well, I didn't either.

I'm not sure what your stand on spirituality and/or God is, but if you allow yourself to be curious as to what and why I bring this up, you'll see where I'm going with this. You never know what you might get out of this spiritual exploration.

For me, spiritual exploration was a game-changer. And it made sense because, if we're made of body, mind, and spirit, and we can be nourishing and taking care of our body and our mind, it stands to reason that properly nourishing our *spirit* is also necessary if we are to operate as a complete being through life. It is the spirit that ultimately makes clearer which path we need to follow in order to feel deeply fulfilled. It leads us where we're meant and *called* to be.

So if you've allowed yourself to be curious and open, let's continue.

Earlier, I mentioned how I would share the first-hand experiences that helped clarify my purpose and calling in life, including the mindset and attitudes that got me where I am today.

One of the elements that acted as a catalyst and helped clarify my direction, my purpose, and my calling, was exploring how spiritual principles could be applied and contribute to my life and business success.

It's in that moment when I decided to give a greater priority and focus to my spiritual development and learn how God works that everything in my life shifted for good. It shifted slowly, but it shifted nonetheless.

Better late than never.

I started to slowly understand how I was—and I believe we all are—called to be part of a greater purpose, which I refer to as God's plan. For my mind to wrap itself around this idea, I simply labeled this greater purpose, *God's plan*, regardless of what I thought I knew or didn't know about God. This in turn led me to think about the idea of calling and purpose in a different way.

Here's what took place in my mind. Brace yourself because I'm going to share my raw and unfiltered thoughts—but first let me reiterate the fact that I personally approach the topic of God from a *spiritual* perspective as opposed to a religious one. Just bear with me and see where I'm going with this. This was where it started:

> *Okay Calling. Me having a calling is me being*
> *"called" to do something. If I'm being called, who is*
> *calling me to do what?*
>
> *And if I'm part of God's plan, doesn't it make sense*
> *that God is calling me to do something for Him?*

A crazy line of questioning? Maybe. But I was willing to explore this idea. Then I wondered:

> *If He's calling me to do something, doesn't it make*
> *sense that I learn about Him and how He works?*
> *This way I'll know how to be guided by Him*
> *because I certainly don't have all the answers. So*
> *how about I go to Him for direction and answers?*

It was in September of 2012 that I decided to start my spiritual experiment by *going within*, using a blend of meditation, prayer, and spiritual readings in hopes of gaining some clarity.

What I didn't know at the time is that what I was actually on a path of fine-tuning was a complete spiritual practice that I've come to call the Peaceful State Process (PSP). It's main benefit—among others—is the deep and sustainable peace one can experience when practicing it daily.

The acquired inner-peace became the pre-requisite to the clarity and sense of direction I needed. If you're interested to learning more about the PSP, visit the resources section at the end of this book.

Going within for direction, using the Peaceful State Process, was the catalyst that helped me get clear on what my *how* (i.e. my vehicle) would be. It became more evident because, instead of relying on my own limited understanding of life, intelligence, and strength, I was nurturing a stronger connection with and reliance on a Higher Power.

By making the choice to solely rely on Him for counsel, it enabled me to better receive, hear, and execute His instructions and guidance.

Since our defined purpose also puts us within the context of a *greater* purpose (i.e., God's plan) why not consider that our purpose is to help realize God's plan? And by His plan I simply mean to make this world a better place.

So in a way, the journey of realizing our purpose, day-in and day-out, can be seen as a process of co-creation, which by default, contributes to us building a stronger connection with God. God being the One we're learning to work with, collaborate with, and create with, as we set ourselves to make a difference around us—a difference according to a plan that satisfies both Him and us at the same time. That's the ultimate process of (divine) co-creation. It is a process at the heart of which lies the spirit of service.

Through the strengthening of this connection we can now be led to make a difference around us in a more meaningful and purposeful way.

As I dove deeper into God's mind so-to-speak—thanks to this spiritual exploration—and my life increasingly became God-centered, I noticed the recurring themes at the heart of the spiritual principles that influence my life moving forward, namely, love and the spirit of service.

Strange concept, don't you think? If this sounds remotely foreign to you, I totally get it. If you feel that way, you simply are where I once was—unable to relate to a concept I hadn't experienced before, didn't understand, and simply wasn't open to yet.

If this is how you feel right now, know that there's nothing wrong about feeling that way. It's normal. And allow me to say that you are exactly where you need to be. Remember how I mentioned earlier that you'd be able to relate to some concepts more than others? I'm just sharing with you what you can most likely expect to experience down the road.

That being said, I strongly recommend going within when looking for direction and being clear on your *how* (your vehicle). And if you have the inclination to suddenly wonder: *Well, how do I do that?* Don't worry. You'll be guided. As you're about to start living a more intentional life that has meaningful purpose, trust and allow yourself to be led through this spiritual experience.

You'll be given the clarity you need to know how to move forward.

Clarity

Sounds obvious but some people don't have clarity, and without it, we can't move forward in the direction that we hope for.

I've found that the ability to find and maintain clarity is a skill that can be harnessed. Even more exciting is the fact that, when done right, it's possible to get timely clarity (almost on command), when we need it. Does this take practice? Absolutely.

The more one spends time nurturing this sense of inner-peace within and bringing their questions into their silent time of introspection—as I've done using the Peaceful State Process—the easier it becomes to receive the needed direction and comfort for that day.

I've also come to realize that the ability to have clarity when needed is made possible when one has inner-peace. To achieve these results consistently, one must commit to make this silent time—which is really our spiritual time—part of our daily (morning) routine.

The purpose journey has a spiritual dimension I strongly recommend you not ignore. Explore it daily and be open to seeing where it'll take you.

Inner-peace is the pre-requisite to clarity.

Some of us would agree that we live in a spiritual world. In this case, why not also learn about the spiritual laws that may affect us as well? Just a thought.

As a side note, expect to hit patches of resistance, which should be expected, whenever we strive to grow spiritually, while choosing to (re)learn about God.

Resistance is normal and should be viewed as an opportunity for growth. Similar to a thick fog that looks like a wall from afar, resistance is the fog that we must, counter-intuitively, push through in order to stretch ourselves both emotionally and spiritually.

Much of the resistance we face is an illusion summoned to make us instinctively feel that we can't or shouldn't push through it so that we back away.

When we find ourselves in a moment of introspection and experience a mental resistance, it's normal to feel as if we should just put a halt to the experience. If we choose to back away, we unfortunately miss on an opportunity to see what we could've learned through having the courage and curiosity to delve deeper into this personal spiritual experience.

I'm sharing this as a way to give you a glimpse of what's to come. It may not make sense now, but in time, as you go through these experiences yourself, you'll know what I'm talking about.

If you've already experienced this, simply consider this a reminder.

Looking inward for clarity is something that I discovered by accident. Again, as a way to let you into my train of thought at the time, I was going from the idea that if God knows and sees all, He could certainly give me a sense of what was ahead. That's why I chose to begin this spiritual experiment by exploring this spiritual path and idea.

I then chose to surrender to this idea and lean more than ever before on Him for counsel. So far, it's worked wonders. It has because it has removed the burden of me having to figure everything out and having to worry about tomorrow. I'm now able to focus on *today*—what I can control today—while keeping my eyes on the future and my aspirations. This is what I call *living today for tomorrow*.

Remember that I committed to sharing with you what has helped me get to a place of clarity regarding my purpose and calling?

The reason why I bring up and advocate for the idea of seriously exploring our spiritual development as the foundation of our lives' true success and fulfillment is that it was the missing ingredient that fast-tracked my own ability route to the clarity I had been looking for all these years.

I believe it can have the same impact on *your* purpose journey. Do we all get to purpose clarity the same way? I'm sure not. All I'm offering is *one* way to get there if whatever you've tried so far hasn't panned out. I strongly suggest being curious about exploring this spiritual path and the idea of relying as well as leaning on our Higher Power in a whole new way.

Remember:

■ To get the clarity we need, we must first have inner-peace as a prerequisite. It's very difficult, if not impossible, to experience clarity without having inner-peace within first.

■ Inner-peace is what allows the voice of clarity within us to make its way to the surface clearly and unfiltered.

That's why it's key to learn how to nurture sustainable inner-peace. The amount of inner-peace that I have experienced over the years since starting this spiritual experiment is nothing I have ever experienced before.

I've practiced various types of meditation before, and most left me feeling more centered but with no connection to our Higher Power, to God. From my own personal experience, the depth and sustainability of peace enjoyed with the self-centered meditation doesn't compare to that which I enjoy today with a more God-centered. Again, this is me sharing my own *personal* experience with the respectful understanding that we all have different spiritual practices that we feel suit us best, and that's perfectly fine.

This peaceful state process has made all the difference in my spiritual grounding in God and has afforded me clearer sense of life direction.

Relying on something bigger than ourselves

When it comes to having direction, we can all agree (I hope) that we can't predict the future and know where we'll exactly end up in life. We can only see so far ahead because of our limited understanding and intelligence. So why not rely on a higher power to guide us?

See, before making that shift, I made the choice to be in control of my own destiny. I did that by removing God from the equation of my life (even though I *believed* in God). I decided that only I would get the credit for my own success.

This approach may work for some, but it certainly didn't work out so well for me. It led me to work harder than I should have and lose everything I thought I had worked so hard to build. I was not getting much *life* traction. If there was any traction, the associated success would be short-lived. Looking back, I feel this happened because—even though I believed in God—I didn't make Him an integral part of my life.

Something I've mentioned before: If He knows all, sees all, and I'm choosing to be an active participant in His Big plan, doesn't it make sense that I lean on Him for guidance, support, and direction?

This is the question I asked myself before committing to let Him be in the driver's seat of my life.

It didn't mean that, all of a sudden, I would not be in control of my life and not make any choices. On the contrary, though I feel that He gives me direction, the gift of free will I have makes me even more responsible for the decisions I make. It still is up to me to make decisions, be accountable for them, and more than ever before, allow myself to be led in the right direction.

This is what it means to be an active participant in our lives, while relying on something bigger than us—which leads us to understanding how to live the best life we can.

We must live the best life we can, not in a way where we chase perfection and the false idea of success, but in a way that leads us to see how much we can stretch ourselves mentally, physically, and spiritually. At the same time, we should strive to serve and support those around us we were called to serve.

This purpose journey is one where I got to learn so much about how we could love life more, love people more, and in the process, came to better understand what really matters in life. It helped me to better understand how life works and to become the best I could be for my own sake and for the benefit others. It afforded me life experience filled with peace, joy, and freedom.

Having God as the number one counsel

What do I mean by having God as our number one counsel?

This was a concept that I was unaware of, and I didn't grasp its meaning at first or the impact it could have in, and on, my life. I didn't fully understand its depth until I reached my tipping point in August 2012 and made the shift that I refer to as the *big decision* where I decided that I would run all my thoughts and decisions-making process through God first. This was no different than the way that some of us run to someone we completely trust when we need a perspective, advice, guidance and support, except I decided to run to Him. This would be my experiment—a spiritual exploration into my life challenges.

At that point in my life, I was tired of being tired because I had worked so hard to build what I *thought* would bring me the success I was seeking in life. I was spinning my wheels and was tired of living my life through trial-and-error. I no longer wanted to live my life relying on my own strength, understanding and limited intelligence because, clearly, it had led me nowhere.

That's why I felt that adopting a new approach was necessary. After all, what did I have to lose?

So I invite you to do the same if what I just shared with you resonates with you or stirred you up inside.

Here's what I can share with you regarding how adopting this way of life has impacted me.

- It's made it easier for me to see what's ahead and coming.

- It's helped me make better decisions in my life—including emotionally difficult ones—and has allowed me to course-correct.

- It has, of course, helped clarify my purpose, my calling, and my next course of action.

Real Life Mechanics
Signpost 3

"Remember: We all get what we can tolerate. So stop tolerating excuses within yourself, limiting beliefs of the past, or half-assed or fearful states. Use your body as a tool to snap yourself into a place of sheer will, determination, and commitment. Face your challenges head on with the core belief that problems are just speed bumps on the road to your dreams. And from that place, when you take massive action—with an effective and proven strategy—you will rewrite your history."

—Anthony Robbins, *Money: Master The Game.*

- Your Dream. Describe it.

- What is your one next step? Set a date to have completed by.

- Explore having God as the driving force in your life. Make the *big decision*. Experiment running all your thoughts and decisions by Him. I invite you to refer to the Peaceful State Process self-guided outline for guided support.

- Nurture inner-peace in order to get the needed clarity when you need it using a complete spiritual practice.

"If you do not change direction, you may end up where you're heading."

—Gautama Buddha.

3. RELINQUISHING UNHEALTHY PURSUITS

Ignoring the tug of the heart.

That moment when we suddenly feel that we want to know what your purpose is. It's felt in our hearts. As if someone has suddenly pulled or even yanked the chain on our heart.

When I started to wonder about that moment, I thought, *Who's doing the pulling and why?*

I believe that each one of us is chosen to carry out a worthwhile mission because of our unique combination of knowledge, skills, and experience. In other words, I believe we all have a unique calling in life, also referred to as a vocation. Though what we do throughout our lives can take many forms, we're only assigned one calling. And it becomes our responsibility to determine what that one thing is.

The moment we open ourselves to this idea and simply follow the fact that our heart is pulling us in that one direction is profound. We must not ignore such moments. We must trust where these feelings can lead us.

In his book *The Soul's Code: In Search of Character and Calling*, James Hillman wrote: "a calling may be postponed, avoided, intermittently missed." Hillman believes that, regardless, the call will eventually get so loud that it can't be ignored. I'd add that, if we ignore the tug of the heart, we run the risk of delaying—or perhaps never accomplishing—something poised to add so much meaning, purpose, contentment, and fulfillment into our lives.

A calling may be postponed, avoided, intermittently missed.

A calling (or vocation) doesn't necessarily need to be something grandiose and out of this world. Our unique calling is the one thing that only we have been designed for. Through our calling, we carry out the one mission that no other human-being can carry out in the way that we can. Regardless of the magnitude of the impact and influence we're meant to have, our mission will look different for each one of us. Even when two individuals may work in the same sphere (business, leadership, coaching, charity, etc.).

Whether it is serving a community, raising a child, helping a person in need, advising clients, or saving the world from extinction, each of us will be entrusted with a sphere of influence within a specific group of people, within a specific environment. Serving *who* and *where* is for us to decide because, remember, we embrace and approach this from the perspective of co-creating with our higher power (in my case, God). We find out, over time, exactly which area we're meant to serve and who we're meant to help.

This discovery process is a continual two-way process where we connect within with our selves in connection to our higher power to get a sense for what we want to do, what we're called to, and what we're meant to do. Then, our responsibility is to go out there and take that one next step that will either move us forward in the right direction or provide a needed course correction. In this latter stage, we still have a choice to make as to what we choose to do next. The burden of responsibility falls on us, not the higher power.

Who's doing the pulling on our heart? I believe our Higher Power, God, is.

I like to believe that when we choose to respond to this call to have a defined purposeful life, we're answering His call to make the world a better place by tackling the problems, the suffering, the deficiencies, that ignite a desire within us to want to do something about it.

We act in response to the pull on our heart.

Where do you feel you're meant to make a difference? What is the one contribution you can see yourself making, and in which arena does it occur? Who are you meant to help? Are they individuals or organizations? What problems, suffering, or deficiencies get you going emotionally? What solutions and insights do you have to offer?

Looking for answers in the wrong places (i.e., externally)

This is something I've been guilty of. Because I didn't know any better, instead of going *inwards*, I spent close to twelve years looking for direction externally through trial-and-error. By externally, I mean I was looking for answers outside of myself in jobs, business opportunities, and even relationships, believing that they'd meet unfulfilled needs.

I should've realized (or have someone tell me) that, since it was a Higher Power, who was yanking the chain on my heart to get my attention, the search for answers was spiritual in nature and that it made sense for me to go inward. Go inward. Connect with Him, and hear what He has to say.

Since the call was a spiritual in nature, I needed to follow a spiritual path to get the answers I sought. This piece of information would've saved me years of frustrations, heartaches, and (most importantly) time.

Of course, this is the path I was meant to take, so I don't have any regrets when it comes to that. At best, I'd consider what we could see as wrong turns simply as detours.

When it comes to the answers I was seeking, because they were spiritual in nature, I had to follow a spiritual path in order to find them, and this was information I was not ready to hear at the time.

Another thing to consider is whether I was even meant to understand all this earlier. Perhaps if I'd understood earlier I would not have gathered necessary experiences and lessons that came from my struggles to understand.

See how life works? The way my life circumstances unfolded occurred for a reason. This book is a perfect example. There are no coincidences. Life events happen for a reason, in a timely fashion, in due time, at the right time, in God's timing. The same is true for you and your life. The only difference lies in how we interpret events and live our lives. We either live life on autopilot (with our heads down and no purposeful context) or we live it intentionally with a higher level of awareness.

God's Timing

When it comes to desired outcomes and when they happen in our lives, we can go about it two ways. One way brings unnecessary stress, frustrations, worry, and fear to overwhelm our lives. I call this personal timing. The other fills our lives with peace. The first one is when we want things to happen when *we* want it. The latter is when we choose to allow things to happen when they're *meant* to happen. I call it God's timing.

When adopting the personal timing mindset, we end up putting ourselves in a position where we want to control events and force them to happen in the way we think is best rather than allowing them to take their natural course. Doing so suggests that we want to control—whether consciously or unconsciously—all aspects of our lives.

A healthier, more empowering approach—one that helps us relinquish control over the things we can't control regardless of our desire to do so—is when we choose to align with God's timing. In this position, we embrace the fact that, because we're part of God's Plan, He knows best when certain events ought to happen.

He's the One that orchestrates events perfectly. Or as I like to say, *God takes care of the details.* Do we all have to believe in that? No. But we can choose to operate our lives that way. The benefit of embracing this mindset includes freeing up a great deal of mental space and pressure in our mind.

That's because we don't have to worry about *when* and *how* events are supposed to take place. We can simply focus on what's on our plate today. This allows us to focus on the things that matter and accomplishing the one task that will get us closer to our goals, *today.*

By aligning with God's timing, you are choosing to trust that, when it comes to the ever-evolving design our lives, His design is better than ours could ever hope to be. This in turn creates the needed space in our lives to simply enjoy our own lives, both logistically and emotionally. This is what a God-centred life looks like.

Does that mean that we won't have moments where we wish things happen sooner? No. Of course we will! It's in our nature as human beings to have these tendencies. The difference moving forward is that, whenever we catch ourselves feeling that way, we can easily remind ourselves about God's timing. He knows best how our events are supposed to unfold. He is taking care of the details. These truths snap us back to the present so that we can enjoy life as it is today.

The choice as to how we want to operate in life is, of course, our own. That's the beauty of having free will.

So how do *you* choose to proceed?

Not asking the right questions.

As I mentioned earlier, I'm sharing a different approach to life. It is a God-centered approach to building a fulfilling life as a purpose-driven person.

The perspectives and mindsets resulting from this different approach to living life have helped me experience, on a daily basis, a profound and sustainable inner-peace, purpose clarity, and fulfillment. These are all things I had been unsuccessfully seeking on my own, and they are now aspects of my life I grate- fully cherish and treasure.

Did it happen overnight? No. It took work and commitment. I was lost and felt like I was running around like a chicken with its head cut-off. I had no clear sense of direction—though I was looking for one—because I was not asking (myself) the right questions.

How could I?

Not only did I not have the right people and mentors around me to highlight what kind of questions I *should* ask myself, but my level of awareness couldn't facilitate the level of pointed intro- spection I needed to have. It wasn't anybody's fault. It just was.

I've found that asking the right life-changing questions comes down to the level of awareness we possess. How can we know how to ask the right questions if we don't even know what we should be asking about in the first place.

Since I didn't know that answering the call on the purpose journey was, in fact, answering God's call—that yanking on chain of my heart—how could I even know to ask more God-centered questions that would lead me inward rather than outward?

This line of questioning is what led me to better understand the Big Plan and how He wanted me to help contribute to it with my unique combination of strengths, skills, and experience.

The same is for you. I feel that you're being called to co-create your life with Him as well. You're being called to serve the world around you in the unique way that only you can. And as Marie Forleo, host of MarieTV and founder of B-School, says, "The world needs that special gift that only you have."

Enough said.

If you're reading this book, I'm willing to bet that you know that you're meant to do something special with your life. You have felt that that you're meant to do something meaningful, impactful, even significant. Whether you have an idea of what that is or not, the fact that you have this feeling is a great place to start. All you need to do now is see where your curiosity will take you.

Allow it to drag you down the spiritual rabbit hole and remember that the answers you seek are *spiritual* in nature. The more you allow yourself—through questions that emerge from the depth of your heart—to follow the spiritual path down this hole, the more answers you'll receive. Allow yourself to be dragged down so you can hear the Voice. Trust.

Once I allowed myself to be pulled down my own spiritual rabbit hole, I was finally understand the mission I felt He was entrusting to me... should I choose to accept it (this one is for the *Mission Impossible* fan out there).

When I talk about mission, I simply mean the responsibility we've been given to make a difference in the world around us, among a specific group of people, in a specific environment—the type of difference that contributes to the well-being of those people in a way that creates more good in the world.

This means offering solutions and support to those we're called upon to help based on what we are passionate about and our core strengths, gifts, and unique perspective. This is what we're meant to do: it's our calling.

The tipping point

What is the tipping point? In the context of the purpose journey, it's an event that has a destructive ripple effect on all areas of our lives, deeply impacting us emotionally and spiritually and leading us to reassess ourselves, our lives, and the direction we're headed.

The tipping point comes in different forms. It can be in the form of an illness, an unfortunate financial event, a broken relationship, and so forth.

For me, it was a promising relationship that was leading to marriage. It was an experience that was filled with hope and excitement because it would've have been the icing on the cake in terms of having everything I could hope to have at that time. I thought I had someone I was going to build the rest of my life with. I had a video marketing business that I was getting off the ground and the building momentum was allowing me to do creative work I enjoyed. I was living in a friendly, beautiful neighborhood in Vancouver, BC Canada, one of the most beautiful cities in the world. Life was good.

Unfortunately, one thing I *didn't* see coming was the fact that the promising relationship would slowly turn into vinegar when my partner would start exhibiting unhealthy behavioral tendencies over a period of a few months. It started with a few physical incidents that ranged from hitting to grabbing, shoving me against walls. When those got addressed, the physical incidents morphed into unhealthy communication ranging from put downs to name calling. And with her anger becoming increasingly difficult to deal with, I chose to break off the engagement. These unfortunate series of events happened over the course of a few months. They didn't happen every day, but they happened often enough that, once I got out of this relationship, I realized I'd had a glimpse of what people in possible abusive relationship go through, especially women. I wish this on no one.

The break up was unfortunately messy, and its aftermath found me back in Edmonton, a city I had left a few years back planning never to return, except to visit family and friends. I found myself at the lowest point of my life wondering why was this happening to me?

> *I work hard, and I'm a good person, so why is this happening to me? I'm thirty-three and I have nothing to show for the last ten years. I have no money, no job, no relationship. I'm in debt and living with my parents again. What am I going to do. Where is my life headed?*

I was still licking my wounds from what I been exposed to in the tail-end of my relationship. I felt like a loser. I was emotionally and spiritually broken and felt alone—even though my family and a few friends were wonderful through this difficult time.

Here I was, back at square one—actually I was standing in a hole somewhere *below* square one—feeling as though I was staring up at a mountain that was so steep and so high its summit was lost in the clouds. I was utterly discouraged. This was my tipping point.

Why did I share this story with you?

First, I believe that, if we don't live life in a way that's aligned with principles that ensures the sustainability and success of our initiatives, it doesn't matter how good and hard-working we *think* we are—what we build will come crashing down.

Second, I suggest viewing a tipping point as a warning sign telling us that what we've been doing up to that point is not working and that, if we don't take decisive action to do something differently moving forward, we shouldn't be surprised to get the same results or maybe worse. I also feel that it be embraced as an opportunity to take a deep look at who we are (mentally, emotionally, and spiritually). We should reflect on how we can start to live not just for ourselves but for others as well and what our purpose and calling in life are. It took a year for me to lay the emotional and spiritual foundation for what my life is like now.

Third, in the aftermath of the tipping point, we have a choice to make. Ignore our circumstance and continue to make the same choices that have led us to experience a tipping point and accept defeat and play the victim; or look at it for what it is and be willing to make *different* choices and learn a different approach to building the life we envision having. This latter choice means we need to be resilient and roll-up our sleeves in order to make it happen.

Naming our Higher Power

Hindsight might be 20/20, but foresight too can be relatively sharp and clear when we choose to rely on and trust something greater than ourselves to lead the way and guide us. That's why I suggest plugging into a greater power for guidance. This choice naturally calls for choosing to consciously learn about about Its inner-workings and how to be one with It. For when we do, our level of intuition, awareness, and clarity is raised to levels that makes managing our present and future life circumstances a more enjoyable process.

Think of it as having a GPS navigation system that allows you to see what's ahead and guides you to a destination that you've never been to before. How much of a sense of peace, relief, and enjoyment does this add to your driving experience and journey? The same applies when choosing to see God as our GPS navigation system.

I can tell you that, when I chose to rely on Him that way, a greater sense of peace, relief, and joy was added to my life experience. Could I have imagined that things would work out that way? No, because it's something that I had never experienced before. Others could have described to me the same picture as I'm doing it with you right now, and I would've understood what they were saying, but I would not have gotten it.

This is one of those things that we must experience first-hand to get it. The same goes with you if you haven't experienced it yet. But you can. You can if you choose to adopt some of the mindsets I've shared with you and even choose to see how the Peaceful State Process (PSP) can help you experience what I'm talking about.

Talking about mindset, the first thing I would encourage you to do, if you're willing to go through the same spiritual exploration I went through, is to look at our Higher Power as a person and give Him a specific name (not something vague as universe as I'll explain why below).

Because of how our brain works, it needs to have something tangible that it can latch onto so it can better focus, the same way it does with someone who we know by name.

There's an interesting mental, emotional, and spiritual chain reaction that get started when our brain associates a name to a higher power. The main benefit is how we get engaged on all levels of our being to nurture an intimate relationship with Him.

It's in our make-up to want intimate relationships. Intimate relationships being the result of getting to know someone at deeper levels over time, while deepening a sense of belonging. So why would that inner-need (even unconscious one) to nurture an intimate relationship with a Higher power be any different if we believe that there is one?

But this can't be done if we don't give our brain a specific name on which it can focus. It's no different that knowing someone by name but knowing nothing about them. It simply makes them a stranger. And He can also be a stranger to us—He certainly was for *me* at one point of my life.

My suggestion, if we are to explore the idea of having a Higher power guide us on this path where we want to see our purpose and calling in life clarified, is to nurture an intimate relationship with Him by first giving Him a specific name. You simply can't have the same sort of relationship with a vague concept.

But if, from the onset, we assign a name to the Higher power, our inner-wheels are designed to snap into motion and engage us in wanting to know more about Him and the Truth we seek. Whether we feel that we know the Higher power or not. The choice of attributing a specific name opens the door to a process of getting clearer answers as to who He is, how we relate to Him, and how we fit in this world. And isn't this the Big question that some of us have and seek answers for?

That's why I suggest training our brain to see God as a person. Regardless of whether someone knows, doesn't know, or can't understand God. Helping our brain process Him as a person is the starting point. A person we can get to know intimately, a person we can have an inner-dialogue with. All other answers that will help us better understand Him, life, and ourselves, will follow later.

This journey that we're on includes, among other things, getting to know what the Higher Power is about at the deeper level and experiencing Him in ways we simply can't imagine yet.

Patience and the desire to understand

I can share with you that the process for getting to know God so is simple. All I've been using since I started my spiritual experiment back in the fall of 2012 is what I'm now calling the Peaceful State Process (PSP).

When we have a desire to better understand how the Higher Power works, there needs to be an understanding that this is a process that takes time. There is only one thing that gets in the way of us experiencing how this learning process will impact our lives, mind, body, and spirit over time: Ourselves—our natural tendency to want to see fast-results, thinking that we know so much more than we actually do, and wanting earth-shattering proof we feel will *make* us believe.

Unfortunately (and fortunately), I've come to realize and feel that He doesn't work that way and has nothing to prove. But I know that He can show you—as He showed me—how your life can be as fulfilling as any you could hope for if only you allow yourself to see where this spiritual exploration can lead.

We forget that our lives are enormous ocean-going vessels that can only be slowly turned. For this reason, patience essential when choosing to allow Him to take the helm. We must follow His charts and sail the routes that He navigates for us.

As I write this book, it has been four years since I reached my tipping point and, after a profound spiritual experience, chose to follow God's lead.

I don't mean to discourage you, but over those four years, for my life to be renewed, I needed to be renewed in mind, body, and spirit. Needful experiences had to be placed on my path so my personal and spiritual growth could be properly nurtured. All this, so I could appreciate, create, and sustain a life filled with a sense of freedom, fulfillment, peace, joy, and of course purpose— a life that I wouldn't trade for the world.

It takes time, my friend. But if you're willing to surrender to the process—if you're willing to trust and be patient—I guarantee that you'll be rewarded in ways you simply can't imagine yet.

Besides, in the grand scheme of things, what's having to invest in a few years, unless you're a quick-learner, when the rest of our lives are poised to benefit?

When you get to that place, you'll see how easy it is to look back and see how your past experiences helped you shape you into the person you're meant to be; how it shaped your ability to make a unique contribution in the lives of those you're called to lead and touch; how it provided the type of experience that's made it easier for you to relate to others and what they're going through. Your past experiences, in short, were there to equip you with what you currently need in order to fulfil the role ahead of you.

Your current situation

Now that you know this, look at your current situation—no matter what it is—as the culmination of experiences that have shaped you to into the person you envision yourself being.

Ask yourself, *how is my current situation shaping me?*

Is it shaping you to excel in a particular area or expand your knowledge regarding a particular topic? Is it challenging in ways that force you to grow or teaching you something about yourself or enlightening you? Is it adding a new skill in your skill box, or simply helping buy time so you can focus on building what you're *meant* to be doing. Everything that happens to us happens for a very specific purpose. It's not random.

Your current situation is there to better equip you to handle what's coming down the road. Whether it's a month, a year, five years, or decades beyond the horizon.

We may not see how it all fits in now—especially if we're going through difficult and *unfair* situations—but as long as we shift our thinking towards how our current situation is meant to help us grow, then no life circumstance can put us down and keep us there forever.

I've had some pretty shitty experiences, and as much as it sucked while I was in the middle of them, I always did my best to quickly get passed thinking of myself as a victim and focus on having faith that good things were coming, that it was temporary, and that there was a *reason* why I was going through this shitty situation.

The difference between one person and another is how they choose to view, interpret, and grow from their past and current experiences.

Our actions and interpretations of life events either condition us to embody a victim mentality or a resilient one. There's no in-between.

Some live out their current experiences by simply going through the motion. Others choose to see opportunities for growth and wisdom that can be capitalized on. Opportunities they see as being within the context of their life's purpose. The latter are intentional, resilient, and growth-focused. These individuals see their current experience as an opportunity to grow and learn about themselves and others while honing a particular skill or deepening their knowledge as it relates to their current situation and the person they're called to be moving forward. That's why I feel that our calling in life is both a privilege and a responsibility.

Growing towards our calling.

The position of CEO is not handed to just anybody. Any candidate who earns such a position has needed to go through various experiences in order to develop the mental capacity, emotional intelligence, confidence, business knowledge and leadership traits needed to handle the responsibility and pressure of the CEO position.

The same goes, I believe, with our calling. The experiences we go through—including the ones we wish we *hadn't* gone through— are there to help us grow into our calling. This is a necessary process designed to equip us in a way that will allow us to successfully carry out our mission because only then will we properly understand the responsibility and pressure of our called position.

That's why I like to frame this growth process as God, life, grooming us for the task He's assigned to us by having us go through the necessary experiences, or (life) training if you will.

Leading, being of service to others, and making a difference in the world is a responsibility and a privilege. Not all respond to that call of course. But for the few that do—and I have a feeling that you're one of them—it's important that they're properly trained for their upcoming privileged responsibility.

When we choose to look at our current situation as training— a stepping-stone if you will—the key thing to remember is that whatever answers or results we seek will come in due time.

There are a couple of reasons for this.

One. We're simply not ready to get the answers we're looking for and, as such, wouldn't be able to handle or understand them.

Two. We must go through a few more experiences that'll help us acquire additional skills or deepens the one we currently have. With our calling being a position of service, responsibility, and leadership, it's only fair that we find ourselves to be competent once it's time for us to help the people (or cause) we've been assigned to serve.

When God sees that we've drawn the right insights from a particular experience and that we're ready to move on to the *next* life experience he'll say, "Level successfully completed! On to the next." It's then that another door then opens and we're on to the next chapter of our lives. When this happens, we must able to recognize the life transition that's taking place and be okay to let go of the previous chapter—as reluctant as we may feel to do so sometimes and as uncomfortable and nerve-wracking a transition may feel.

Looking at our decisions.

Now, what happens when we *don't* successfully complete a level? Well, we get to relive that particular experience in a different way or form. This is where some of us—and I've experienced this as well—have patterns we don't seem capable of escaping. The main reason for this lies with the key decisions we don't realize we need to change when confronted with a particular situations.

An example can be dating situations when someone keeps on being with an emotionally unhealthy partner and having poor dating experiences. Here, a recurring life event is having potential partners presenting themselves. And some potential decisions that may need to be altered could include finding different venues for meeting potential partners, asking more relevant questions earlier on during interactions, or getting to know someone for a longer period of time before committing to being in a relationship with them.

Our decisions are what ultimately shapes both our life experience and what we experience within. And until we start making life-enhancing decisions, we stay stuck on the same level. That's why we must focus on making life-enhancing decisions.

Every life event (every moment) is an opportunity to redefine the quality of our lives through a course correction moving forward. Yes, it happens one step at a time, but the quicker we realize this and start implementing this right away, the sooner our lives will transform into the fulfilling pictures we've tried to reach for all along.

This is when life starts to become fun and can be looked at it as an adventure.

What has helped me is adopting the following life-enhancing mindset when it comes to any life circumstances I find myself in. I ask myself: *"What is life/God trying to teach me through this?"*

This mental framework has helped tremendously.

Once I decided to make this mental shift, this mindset has helped me grow in both patience and humility and focus on what matters, today.

Real Life Mechanics
Signpost 4

If we want different results in our lives, we must be willing to do things differently and explore other options with an open mind.

- Implement life-enhancing decisions.

- Develop the habit of reflecting on how your current situation is preparing you for what's coming.

- Determine what growth opportunities are contained in present situations.

- The answers you seek are spiritual in nature, so go *within* for answers. Allow yourself to be dragged down the spiritual rabbit hole.

- Choose to operate on God's timing and have a God-centered life.

- View God as a person and develop an intimate relationship with Him through dialogue (refer to the PSP to see how I did it).

- Focus on what you can control today while keeping your eyes on where you envision yourself being in the future. Letting God take care of the details. I like to sum this idea up by saying: *Live today for tomorrow.*

"The purpose of life is not to be happy. It is to be useful, to be honorable, to be compassionate, to have it make some difference that you have lived and lived well."

—Ralph Waldo Emerson

4. TAKING GRADUAL POSITIVE STEPS

Looking back at the way my purpose journey began after having my heart tugged over ten years ago, I realize that I actually already knew what my purpose in life was. I knew that I wanted to help people reach their goals while being aligned with their purpose. I simply didn't know exactly what it (my calling) would look like.

I didn't know that my calling would end up being in the form of a spiritual guide, mentor, and author. And this is the challenge that most of us face. The challenge of not knowing what our vehicle (calling) looks like once we figure out our purpose.

The calling (or vocation) is the physical expression or embodiment of our purpose. It also "can refer not only to ways of doing—meaning work—but also to ways of being" according to James Hillman, author of the *Soul's Code*, in an interview with Scott London. As I view purpose and calling one of the same yet distinctive elements, it's still important that we differentiate the two.

In the early stage of my purpose journey, I looked at purpose and calling as one and the same, without differentiating the two. The problem was that when I realized I could finally articulate my purpose but still could not decide on the *vehicle* I'd need to use to fulfil that purpose I was left wondering: *Now what?* I experienced a similar feeling when I was able to refine my purpose, particularly when I determined—in more specific details—*how* I was meant to help others and who they were, more specifically.

So you can imagine if someone hasn't even gotten to the point where they've clearly defined their purpose, how difficult and frustrating it is to figure out what the best so-called vehicle for the job. And with my purpose still undefined, no wonder I couldn't know, for sure, which vehicle to choose.

You may already know in your heart who you want to be and what you want to do.

Unfortunately, as it was with me, what gets in our way are the questions related to how should all the pieces of the puzzle fall together. We put the pressure on ourselves to figure it out. Let me share with you a secret: *There's nothing to figure out*. I'll say it again.

There's nothing to figure out.

You have nothing to figure out because you already *know* what it is you're meant to do. The only thing holding you back is the next step you *know* you must take in order to make your vision a reality.

The choosing of a *vehicle* (i.e. discerning a calling) is the kind of complex equation that our brain loves to focus on, and that sort of focus can drag us into a chaotic, overwhelming, frustrating, problem-solving process. Should we blame our brain? No. After all it's designed to solve problems and find solutions.

My suggestion is simple. Let God takes care of the details.

The only thing you must focus on is completing the next step or task ahead of you. As you move forward, then the picture will get clearer for you, and time will help. Think of it as an automobile assembly line. Does the car look like a car at the beginning of the assembly line? No, but it starts looking more and more like a car as it gets closer to the end of the line.

It's the same with us and our vocational vehicle. As we go through the life assembly line with purpose, our vehicle is assembled a piece at a time as we complete the next course of action, and the next, and the next.

You already are in the process, so instead of focusing so much on what your vehicle should look like (i.e. the final result at the end of the assembly line) shift your focus on the next course of action you need to handle today—the next checkpoint on the assembly line.

Focus on the one that makes you feel energized, excites you, gets your creative juices flowing, fully challenges you, the one you feel your heart is pulling you towards. Focus your energy in moving in *that* direction. The way your vehicle looks like will get clearer and clearer along the way.

Clarifying Purpose.

Our purpose in life comes down to helping and serving others, or a cause, and is what is going to both become and shape our life's work (our calling). It will become our legacy.

But how can we easily determine the answer to this seemingly big question. Well, it only becomes a big question when we look at it that way. It can, however, become a simple question with simple and concrete answers when we choose to look at it that way. It's a matter of perspective.

Clues as to our purpose can be found within us—as mentioned earlier—but also externally. See, for us to be clear on what path to follow on our life's spiritual journey, it's important to look at what's happening around us. This is how we confirm the validity of answers found within.

External clues are the confirmation to our internal answers.

By looking at circumstances around us—whether they be in our personal, professional, or business lives and whether they'd be related to seeing what other people do for a living, volunteering, or simply go through—we can be led to an a-ha moment and say:

"This is what I want to do!"

That a-ha moment is one to pay attention to because it's an unfiltered expression of the heart. An unfiltered expression that clearly reveals to us the path that we must set out on.

Does it necessarily mean that the vehicle you see other people use is the one you'll use? No, not necessarily because the way your vehicle will be assembled is going to be done in a way that's unique to you. The only way you'll know how it'll end up looking is by starting to take the next step, and the next step, and the next.

For now, the important thing is to acknowledge what your heart clearly saw and thus define what it is that you're meant to do.

When you experience that a-ha moment of knowing what you're meant to do—what your purpose is—write it down. Write at the top of your board, the first page of your journal, in your smart-phone, *somewhere* you can see often until you believe it in heart and mind.

Until you believe it *wholeheartedly.*

That is your purpose as it stands today. Expect however, for it to get refined to your core and true purpose over time as you move forward on this journey. This is nothing to be frustrated over just because all that this refinement means is that you are getting increasingly clearer on what your unique contribution in this world as a human being is. It's a reflection of your personal and spiritual growth.

You're now one step ahead of the game because when others feel that their purpose keeps on changing—which may lead them to experiencing increased frustration—you know that *yours* only gets refined over time. And there's a lot of peace and excitement that comes along with realizing this.

So keep your purpose front-and-center in your mind. Whenever you find doubts creeping into your mind as to whether this is really your purpose or not, stir your mind back to your defined purpose until your mind totally buys into it. If we don't do this, it'll be easy for our mind to gravitate towards other shiny objects that will delay our ability to live out our purpose or—worst-case scenario—take us in a direction that will prevent us from fully living it.

If you find that you haven't had that a-ha moment yet, no need to feel discouraged. The fact that you're here reading this book is proof that you're closer than you think to getting the answer you seek. The question of purpose is already in the back of your mind and has been stirring you up inside whether you know it or not.

What's needed now is to shift gears and make this question a more conscious question, one that now directs and influence your decisions moving forward. You want to make that question the fuel of your life engine.

That being said, the answer to this question is not one to be figured out mentally. It simply comes to us from the heart, meaning that we must allow the answer to come to the surface.

We must let our heart do the talking, which can only happen when we set our mind to the side—or put it in neutral—when pondering this question. Some refer to doing this as being *still* or just *being*.

Allow the answer you seek to come to the surface. Let the heart speak.

Write the question where you can see it at all times. Write it so you can easily access it and be prompted to think about it. Once that's done, let go of it and go about day as you normally would—let the answer come to you.

Remember that this is a question that is spiritual in nature, so make time for silent introspection, and take this question in that silent space. While in that silent space, it's important to address the question in towards your (named) higher power, for example:

"God, what is my purpose in life?"

Then let go of the need for an immediate answer and allow it to come to you in due time. Again, the formula is simple: Ask the specific question with, let go of it, and let the answer to swim up to you (from the heart) rather than actively going fishing for it (with your mind).

Now what if someone so happens to not believe in God? Can or should they still ask this type of question?

Whether you believe in God or not, I suggest using a specific name for the Higher Power from whom we seek answers. Asking this question within us is us sending a message to theOone we hope can provide us with answers. It's the same as when we send a message out into space and hope for a response even if we're not sending the message to a specific recipient; the same thing applies here when we send a message to an unspecified recipient in the spiritual realm.

We open the channels of communication when we send in a message within. And as we wait for an answer, an exchange takes place. This is the basis of a dialogue. This is the basis of what a prayer is: a dialogue.

If you don't believe in God, simply trust the process. Set your mind aside and suspend your beliefs about spirituality and God that have been shaped by your past life experiences for the purpose of this different way of finding answers that you know your heart seeks and possibly long for. Allow yourself to be guided by your heart and spirit and simply see where this exploration will take you. The right answers will come to you, but only if your specific questions are pointed in the right direction.

Clarifying the next step.

Once we have determined—or are in the process of determining—what our purpose is, our ability to determine what we should do next is made clearer when acknowledging and focusing on our dream and feelings contained *within* our dream. And when we focus on these elements and follow through with our actions, the chances of creating the fulfilling life we envision having increase.

Purpose + Dream + Feelings (contained within the Dream) + Actions Taken = Fulfilling life with meaningful purpose.

This can also be viewed as a simple formula to fulfill a prophesy: Know the vision, act in a way that confirms it.

Regardless of how we envision our fulfilling life, all the information we need to guide us on this purposeful life journey is contained in our dream. Within our dream are contained the emotions that act as a guiding compass towards the life circumstances and people that will help us make living our purpose a reality.

Success leaves clues like breadcrumbs for us to follow. The question becomes how can we find the right people and mentors who can help us with the unique dream and vision we desire to make reality?

We find those mentors who specialize in helping with the particular need we have today, at this stage of our lives. We also look for those who have achieved the end result we seek and are willing to share with us the wisdom that allowed them to get there. Or we seek out those individuals who can help us transform into the person we see ourselves being.

Mentors enter our lives when we are ready to receive their teachings, support, and guidance. They enter our lives for a season, which can be for a few hours, month, years, or a lifetime.

Regardless, the first thing to clarify *before* looking for a mentor is the nature of our dream. That clarity is the starting point.

By being clear on our dream means being clear on *everything* from what we see ourselves doing, to what we're meant to do (and the lifestyle around that), to the people we want in our lives, the people we want to associate with, the people who will be grateful for the way we're able to impact their lives. It means being clear on the unique contributions we have to offer the people, organizations, the world. Being clear on your dream means knowing, in our heart and mind, what would qualify as a fulfilling life of meaningful purpose.

If you feel that you don't have answers to those different facets of your dream, there is no need to feel discouraged. As you list those different items and keep them in the forefront of your mind and ponder them, the answers *will* come. They will as long as you move in the direction you feel your heart is drawing you. Keep a journal or a smartphone close by so you can easily jot down those answers to what your dream looks like whenever they surface and feel right. They may come to you bit by bit—like small pieces of a puzzle. But in time, you'll get the full picture.

You are fine right where you are.

With as little or as much as you know about your dream, ask yourself:

> "What kind of support would I need from a mentor or coach as it relates to my purpose and my dream?"

Take the time to think about it. Allow answers to come from within versus trying to figure it out with your mind.

The answers that surface are the crumbs to follow. They will point you in the right direction when it comes to knowing which type of mentor you need right now, what type of book you need to read, what kind of workshop or training program you need to sign-up for, what new life experience you should go after, who you should meet for coffee.

The answer always either leads to one next course of action to focus on, or confirms that the direction we're taking is the right one.

The process is simple:

- Go within for answers

- Wait for answers to surface

- Take action as prescribed by the answers

- Wash–rinse–repeat.

So again, once you're clear on what your purpose is—or once engaged in the process of knowing what it is—be increasingly clear on what your dream is. Let your emotions guide you where you're meant to be. Look around for people with personal, professional, business, or charitable accomplishments you resonate with. The heart doesn't lie. When the heart sees it, it knows, and you'll know. When you catch yourself thinking, *I'm going to be like one of them*, you are on the right track. This concept is not new, I know. But just like any concepts that aren't new, it's worth mentioning them as reminders.

Fully trust the good direction your heart is pulling you towards. As a word of caution, we should expect our brain to play interference by way of thoughts that sow fear and doubt.

As purpose-driven individuals, we constantly face this challenge. That's why we need to learn how to become heart-driven as opposed to head-driven. If we are to apply the 80/20 rule, being head-driven would be us using our head 80% of the time and our heart only 20% of the time when making decisions. My recommendation is to flip this ratio and be heart-driven with heart/head being 80/20.

We must learn to be heart-driven more than head-driven.

I suggest leading with our heart and use it as our life compass for direction. Our head should preferably only be used to problem-solve how to efficiently execute a task or go about finding the needed opportunities or encounters to help reach our next goal. The heart sets the course, our mind figures out the most efficient way to reach our destination.

Often, we rely on our mind to both set the course and figure out the most efficient way to reach our destination. When this happens, we find ourselves without real direction, for only our heart has the true coordinates we're meant to move toward. For this reason, we must be vigilant in reminding ourselves that our heart and head have two complementary and distinctive functions.

Without consulting our heart, we become directionless and dreamless.

A purpose within a purpose.

Everything in life has a context. When things are taken out of context, we remove the meaning of their existence and their purpose. The same things applies to our lives. That's why it's important to think of what the larger context of our lives is.

Without context, our lives have no meaning. And without meaning, our lives have no purpose. For our lives to have purpose, they must have meaning. And for lives to have meaning, they must also have context. It is then that we can experience the peace, contentment, and fulfillment we've been longing for all along.

When we choose to look at our lives as being ones that fit within a greater context, the trick becomes knowing what that context is. The same applies for our life's purpose. Our life's purpose is a purpose within a (greater) purpose.

Remember me alluding to God's Big Plan, the context, and how our purpose fits within His grand purpose earlier?

This perspective is one that can also help us better decipher our own purpose. It is one that I encourage all of us to explore. Here's why.

Doesn't it make sense to see how our purpose helps serve the greater good? A purpose that ties into God's ultimate desire for a better world, a world where there's less suffering, more peace, more good, more love for one another, a world where we leave it better than we found it?

For that to become true, He needs our help. He calls us to help Him with this important task. I firmly believe that we're called, that He recruits us by assigning us a calling so we can contribute by individually making a difference in the world. So why not answer that call for such an honourable and worthy (divine) cause?

We are called to make a difference on earth in order to make the world a better place. And once we accept the idea that our Higher Power, God, in a desire for co-creation, calls us to make a difference, the next logical step—it seems to me—is to learn as much about our *caller* as possible.

Using what I have come to call the Peaceful State Process (PSP), I did just that, and when I did, the deeper and clearer my sense of mission became. It was then that the process of leading a God-centered life took root for me.

Going through this same process doesn't require that you believe in God. I say this because, as I started this spiritual experiment and exploration, I went in curious to see if this God-centered approach would really make a difference in my life—to the point that if it hadn't panned out, I'd have left the idea of God behind and walked away.

That's why I say that it doesn't matter whether you believe in God or not. All that I invite you to do—as I felt I was invited to do (by Him)—is to give this different approach a shot. It simply is a mindset that, once adopted, will naturally draw you towards the things that will help you create and maintain a fulfilling life that has greater meaning and purpose.

That's why I'm emphasizing the idea of nurturing our spiritual development as the foundation for success in all areas of our lives.

Now, if we're choosing to *align with God* for the purpose of this experiment, then we also have a responsibility to get to know how He works and how life works so we can best answer the call, don't you think? Isn't this what we do anyway with our boss at work, people we collaborate with, or people we answer to?

To get to that place of better understanding how He/Life works, we need the right (spiritual) tool. For me, the Peaceful State Process is both the tool and the process I underwent over the last few years, and it has been instrumental in helping me better understand how the Higher Power and life works.

To better understand how God and life work, we need the right spiritual tool.

I go into more details as to how it can be as instrumental in impacting your life in ways you can't imagine in the complimentary self-guided outline available for download. You can download it once you subscribe for my newsletter at www.RealLifeMechanics.com.

The PSP has impacted both my life and my *self* in surprising ways I couldn't have foreseen when starting this spiritual exploration. It has also afforded me a deeper understanding of what it means to be the leader I see myself being. It helped show me how to be whole, how to be emotionally free, how I fit in this world, how to focus on today, how to be a better human being, and how to better be of service to others in a way that perfectly aligns with my core strengths, desires, and aspirations.

Most importantly, this spiritual tool helped me grow into the person I needed to become—and was called to be—so that I could successfully carry out my mission through my calling. It was the catalyst that facilitated my transformation on a mental, emotional, physical, and spiritual level.

In case you're wondering, I practice the PSP on a daily basis and it is still helping me grow. It helps me learn something new every day about people, life, my core strengths, my emotions, love, commitment, people, developing a stronger guided intuition, healing, my one item of focus for the day based on the area of my life that needs the most attention, true freedom, life, and of course God. It's a beautiful thing.

A simple purpose equation.

As I adopted a God-centered perspective to this concept of purpose, I was led to this simple question.

What's another way to look at what purpose is?

The answer I came up with was this:

Our purpose is the act of helping create more good and less suffering around us and in our world. With "world" having different meaning for all of us. It could represent the organization we feel could operate so much better if only (fill in the blanks), the neighborhood that could feel much safer if only (fill in the blanks), the families that could get through difficult times if only (fill in the blanks), the individual whose well-being could be raised if only (fill in the blanks). "World" is where you're called to make a difference.

Real Life Mechanics
Signpost 5

When searching for purpose, we're in fact looking for the type of work—our life's work—that we can single-mindedly focus on. This is work that will ultimately be what we'll be known for in our circles and/or in the world. This life's work is ultimately our legacy and will be left behind once we're gone.

- Trust that moment of absolute clarity when realizing what your purpose is.

- The desire to make a difference and help people is the reflection of our purpose. Focus on it.

- Let the heart set the direction and the mind problem-solve getting there.

- Find the right mentor for what's needed at this point in time. Emulate the best yet blaze your own trail.

- Put your life and work into a greater context in order to give it greater meaning and purpose.

- Focus on learning how the One and life works. Have a God-centered life. This helps make it easier for us to see how we fit in the grand scheme of things.

4. TAKING GRADUAL POSITIVE STEPS

"There is no greater gift you can give or receive than to honor your calling. It's why you were born. And how you become most truly alive."

—Oprah Winfrey

Each one of us will get to live out our purpose in a way that's unique to us. It is our one thing. To determine what that one thing is, we must look first at what people naturally come to us for and what is that we offer that impacts others the most—while bringing us the highest level of satisfaction and growth—based on our core strengths, abilities, unique experience, and passion. That's our one thing.

Dealing with multiple passions.

Based on what I just said—and revisit this as needed—what do *you* feel is your one thing? Remember to allow the answer to come from within instead of trying to figuring it out with your mind. You'll know when the right answer comes up. You'll feel it to the core.

Think about the things you do that cause you to think:

> *I love this...*
> *I could do this all day...*
> *This always gets my creative juices flowing...*
> *This is when I feel most alive...*
> *I get such a charge out of this...*
> *This never even feels like work...*

Some will say that it is your passion, which is possible. But I would say that not all passions are created equal. As someone who wants to do what they love—and probably wants to earn a full-time income doing it—choosing to focus on the right passion is key.

Some passions don't allow us to be in our sweet spot where we focus our energy on what we're best at and what differentiates us from the next person. This is because they're aren't what I refer to as the *primary* passion.

The primary passion is the one that links up to our purpose and our natural core strength, talent, or gift. It is a reflection of how we see ourselves now and in the future. It is what we absolutely love doing and what brings us the most joy.

We hear people say (and I've experienced that as well), "I have so many passions that I don't know which one to choose!"

My suggestion is to find the primary passion that will help you earn that full-time time income. The other secondary passions, fall into either hobbies or passions that will help support fueling the primary one.

Using myself as an example, my passions include writing, mentoring, shooting videos, interviewing people, travelling, fitness, giving people advice, attending conferences, branding and marketing.

So out of all of them, which one should or did I choose as my primary passion?

Writing.

Why writing? As someone who has aspired, since my college days, to entrepreneurship, I had to go through the journey to figure this one out. Writing is at the heart of my business because it's what I absolutely *love* doing.

I love it because I get to do what comes easily to me, which is to put my ideas down on paper. I love thinking about them, learning about them, studying them, analyzing them, and sharing them because I feel I have something to share with the world that I deeply believe can make a difference. As my primary passion, writing is also a form of creative expression for me. It is a full expression of who I am.

So I see myself as a writer and present myself as a writer. When I see other accomplished authors out there, my soul identifies with them and recognizes itself as belonging to that tribe of individuals.

As a writer, the books that I publish become the vehicle that helps me carry out the one thing (mission) I was called to do as a writer (my calling), which is to help people clarify and live their purpose (my core and true purpose), so they can define their calling, and claim the fulfilling lives that they're meant to have (the desired outcome for those I feel called to serve).

On to you now. And this is something you may need to revisit overtime but at least you'll have a framework to work with:

As a [_____], the [_____] that I [_____] become(s) the vehicle that helps me carry out the one thing (mission) I was called to do as a [_____] (my calling), which helps people [_____

_____

__] (my purpose) so they can [_____] (the desired outcome for those you feel called to serve).

Now how about the secondary passions? They either fall into the hobbies category or they are the support cast to the primary passion. For example:

My business is called Real Life Mechanics, and you'll notice when visiting my website (www.RealLifeMechanics.com) how I've managed to integrate some of my secondary passions.

- Branding. See how the website is laid out and the details behind its design (shout out to Leanne from www. ShiftDesigns.ca)

- Promoting and getting to know interesting people, their stories, and how they make a difference, on video. (see the interviews on my blog)

- Travelling for business and sharing my insights in front of crowds (when attending conferences and events)

- Marketing and building relationships (through my news-letter and networking)

- Working privately with clients, seeing their transfor-mation, and helping them get to where they envision themselves being as a purpose-driven individuals (visit the "Clarity" tab on my website to see what the Clarity Sessions has done for those who've experienced it)

These are all secondary passions that help fuel my business, experience, and primary passion of writing. As they work cohesively, I now am in the best position to help people, including you, uncover the one thing that they can finally focus on for the long-term. The one thing that will help them build the legacy that they'll leave behind and be remembered for.

Focus on your primary passion, find the supporting cast (secondary passions), and let the rest be hobbies.

Serving others.

If you find yourself still struggling with the question of your purpose and calling in life, the answer might be closer than you think. I say this because the answer can be found in our desire to serve others or the way that we already help those around us, even if it's the something we do for free.

Another way to get some answers is to look in the rear-view mirror of our lives. In other words, our past.

Our past personal experiences or the ones we've witnessed others go through—whether they are profound, traumatic, struggling, or deeply moving experiences—are signposts pointing us to the things that we may feel very passionate (or obsessed) about. The things that fire us up emotionally.

When we look back, it becomes easier to see patterns of who tends to gravitate towards us, who we naturally attract and come to us for support, the type of environment we tend to gravitate towards, what topics feel natural to talk about (all day), and what experiences have brought us the most joy and fulfillment.

Patterns aside, if those past experiences ignited a strong desire to want to help others and do more of that, then this is a good sign that you have something to offer to a particular group of people. This group of people is who you're called to lead, develop, motivate, inspire, bring hope to, provide comfort to, or alleviate the suffering of, whatever the case may be.

If you have learned from these experiences and found a genuine desire to make a difference in the lives of those who could learn from you, then you are the person others will look up to for guidance, wisdom, and direction. This is the area where you're meant to serve.

A likely challenge that you'll now face is not whether you'll accept this role, but rather whether feel *worthy* of leading others that way.

> *Why me? Who am I to lead others that way? Why would others pay me for this? There are so many*

other people that I know who are so much better
than me...

This is a typical response when we are confronted with the opportunity to step into what we're called to do—*especially* when there's the possibility of getting paid to do it.

If this doesn't apply to you, fantastic! But if this is you, remember that you are called to carry out a specific task that requires your unique combination of skills, experience, and way of seeing the world. That's why only you can carry out this unique mission. If you don't, the world is simply missing out on your unique contribution and the difference you can make.

Claim who you are and what you've been called to do. Let time, people, and the world confirm how valuable you are to them. Your responsibility is simply to get to work, starting today, and letting more people know how you help others or organizations.

Accumulated knowledge and unique experience.

Those of us who are called to lead significant, meaningful, and purposeful lives leading others are chosen because of our above-average knowledge of a topic we happen to also feel passionate about.

Of course, I believe that we all have a calling. I also believe that not all of us choose to answer the call or even care to answer it. That being said, here's another way to look at the relationship between our purpose and calling in life:

Our purpose is helping people (or organizations) who are experiencing a struggle that we've already experienced first-hand or have witnessed. By sharing our experience and understanding, we can alleviate people's (or organization's) brokenness. We can improve their lives (or the way they operate) by offering a unique solution made possible by our particular combination of our life's experience, accumulated knowledge, core strengths, and skill sets.

So what do you *feel*—not think—your purpose is?

Don't worry about nailing it the first time. Simply jot down your best answer as a way of starting the process; you'll be able to refine your answer over time as you go through life and amass work experience (so long as you revisit this question regularly).

A few questions that will point you in the right direction.

What is a struggle that you've witnessed—or maybe one you've experienced yourself—for which you now have hard won answers and insights? Is this a struggle you still absolutely identify with? Did you yourself overcome this struggle? Can you see yourself helping others overcome it?

What vehicle (calling) can you use to help improve someone's life or help them get what they want based on your own experience? Do you have you a book in you? Are you musically inclined? Can you produce movies, organize events, build a company with a social agenda?

To get some ideas, remember that you can look externally at people who are already making a difference in the social, business, or charitable arenas that interest you. There's nothing wrong with thinking, *Hey I could do that too.* You will bring your own skills and experiences to any project.

Real Life Mechanics
Signpost 6

Believe in who you are and what you have to offer. Let the world know because the world awaits.

- Look at patterns in your past to determine who naturally comes to you for support. They are who you're meant to lead and support.

- Claim who you are as the go-to-person for what you believe is a worthwhile cause to pursue.

- Look at what you've personally experienced or have witnessed in your past that has given you an above-than-average understanding of the matter. This is what others will come to you for. Focus on this one thing. This is your area of expertise.

- Look into your heart and discover what you feel strongly about. That's your drive for wanting to make a difference.

"Only he who keeps his eyes fixed on the far horizon will find his right road."

—Dag Hammarskjöld

5. LOOKING AHEAD

When it comes to getting ourselves to a foreign destination for the first time, isn't it so much easier to get there when we're giving a roadmap to follow or can plug the destination coordinates into a GPS navigation system?

I wish someone had shared with me what to expect as I got on this purpose journey in early 2000. That's why I've put together what I've noticed to be the different stages of this unique journey and quest for fulfillment. Is it the be-all and end-all of how this journey goes? No. But it can at least provide a few reference points so the journey ahead can be a little smoother and you can find peace in knowing that you're on the right track or know when to course-correct.

Let's dive in, starting with what can delay the progress we hope to make on this purpose journey.

Things to look out for include:

A. Forgetting to look for answers within. This leads us to look for answers in the wrong places.

B. Forgetting what our purpose is once we've discovered it.

C. Not having our purpose as a primary drive in our lives when we haven't defined it yet.

D. Wanting to rush the process of knowing how our purpose will translate into a calling and what our vehicle is going to look like. This more than anything will create unnecessary frustration.

E. Not striving to design a lifestyle that will *support* creating the life we feel we're meant to have. If we have a 9-5 job, our lifestyle needs to effectively support our purpose ambitions as a side project.

F. Overthinking what carrying out our mission through our calling ought to look like. Remember, God takes care of the details.

G. Not being mindful of the time gap between knowing what our purpose is and being able to live it out through our calling. Or (the other way around) by knowing and living our calling but not having been able to put it within the context of a lucid purpose yet. The speed at which one can bridge this time gap will vary from one individual to the next. Building these kinds of bridges requires one to be patient and process-focused (rather that results-focused).

H. Being results-focused versus process-focused. We must learn to enjoy the journey for its own sake. We must understand that, on this journey, we are purpose-driven and that what we're doing today contributes to our needed development. That development ensures that we grow into the person we need to be in order to be ready, once the time comes, to be called to fully carry out our mission through our calling.

I. Not regularly checking our alignment between God's Big Plan (the greater Purpose), our purpose, our (God-centered) life, our mindset, our choices, and our actions.

J. Trying to build our lives and create our success on our own, while taking our spiritual development and the co-creating of our lives with the One out of the equation. To each their own, but as I tried that myself, this path led to my tipping point. I'm never going back there again, as I find myself cracking a smile and shaking my head thinking about it.

Stages of the purpose journey.

Looking back at purpose journey that I embarked on over a decade ago, I've noticed distinct stages. You may recognize yourself as being in one of these stages. This will make it easier to know how to best proceed and what to set you mind to. Focus on a simple roadmap that can be followed.

You'll find that there are different checkpoints on this purpose journey. If you have any question regarding the different stages or questions related to other parts of this book, be sure to let me. You'll find my contact information in the resources section of this book.

Here are the different stages of the purpose journey.

- **Stage One**: Going through the motions of life.

Not knowing that we have a purpose, not looking for it, and maybe not even caring to have one or believing that we have a purpose.

We simply go through the motions of life.

- **Stage Two**: The Pull.

Something awakens something in us that makes us realize that we want to know what our purpose is, and our heart is tugged. For some reason, we feel that there's more to life than the path we're currently on.

For some, years can go by before doing something about what they felt in their heart—as the saying goes, *Life happens*.

Most of us rely more on our head that on our heart.

At this stage, we're not aware of the distinction between purpose and calling. They are one of the same.

- **Stage Three**: The Search (Part one)

We intensely seek to figure out what our purpose is, but we don't know how to go about it.

We typically experience frustrations and heartaches. It's a difficult stage because we go look for answers and can't seem to find them no matter how hard we try or who we go to for advice.

We look for answers in the wrong places (externally) and still can't get the answers we seek. The feeling that we're not meant to have what we refer to as average lives intensifies. By average—because we can't find the right vocabulary—we mean a life without meaning and most commonly travelled by the masses. We feel that we are different and want something different in our lives.

Relationships often get affected at this stage, and promising long-term relationships fall apart.

Some can experience their tipping point at this stage with their world—the result of years of blood, sweat, and tears (extreme, I know, but you get the point)—coming crumbling down.

We start feeling that we're not on the right career path. People around us don't *get* us. Starting to feel alone on this journey is not uncommon.

Financially, cutting down expenses to the bare minimum may be required.

Emotionally speaking, we may have to go through a healing process and let go of the things that are holding us back.

Some of us may start to rely more on our intuition when it comes to how we choose to live our lives. A greater interest in spirituality develops.

Spiritually speaking, we may not be too sure as to the role of our spiritual development will play in our ability to live on purpose and create the fulfilling and successful life we envision.

■ <u>Stage Four</u>: The Search (Part two) & Spiritual Awakening.

We've figure out what our purpose is but then realize that we don't know how to go about living it out. In other words, we don't know what our calling (or vehicle) is. We're now looking to define our calling, the physical expression of our purpose.

We come to realize that purpose and calling are different things and the search to figure out what our "calling" is begins.

Frustration ensues and time does not seem to go fast enough. Thoughts about others being so much further ahead of us in life start creeping into our mind, and we start questioning how successful we really are. We might be in the process of rebuilding our lives at this point.

Questions regarding how to integrate ideas, passion, and our purpose into what we feel we are meant to do fuels our need to know how to make it happen.

We may fall victim to comparing ourselves with our peers or people we think are more successful than us. We may still doubt our ability to be successful and even whether we have something of value to offer in a way that's authentic.

From a life standpoint, we become better at choosing who we let into our lives and start focusing on what really matters. We start to streamline our lives, and big changes tend to happen in our lives. Changes that sometimes are out of our control.

Relationships we thought would stand the test of time *don't*. Unexpected friendships surface and deepen. More than before, we shift from focusing on quality rather than quantity in all areas of our lives, from relationships, to the way we eat, to opportunities, *all* areas of our lives get affected one by one and possibly re-evaluated.

Emotionally speaking we may be ready to step into the *new us* that's more grounded emotionally and spiritually.

The transition from our old life to the new one happens with a bit of turbulence. Like an old house being torn down so that a new one can be built on the same spot, elements of our old life are being tore down, one by one, or repurposed. From relationships (break up, divorce), to jobs (quitting or being fired), businesses (having to fold it, go through a round of firing, rebranding), nothing is spared. It's an unfortunate part of the process but one we must recognize and have the courage to accept it and go with it.

Spiritually speaking, some of us make the choice to do what we can to reorient our spirituality and God at the center of our lives as the force driving our lives. We choose to do this by following

His lead and aligning with the Him, (re)learning to understand how He and life works. We become more curious about real-life mechanics. For some, this is a time of spiritual awakening.

We become better at trusting as well as relying on our intuition and spirit. At this point, it's more heart and less of our head driving the ship of our lives.

■ Stage Five: Claiming and owning who we are.

We finally realize what our calling is in relation to our purpose!

At this stage, we now know what our calling is in relation to our purpose. Now the fun begins.

We claim our unique and core identity. We're ready to present ourselves to others in a way that's true to ourselves, in an authentic way.

The fun begins because it's now time to utilize our core strengths, gifts or talents, while honing our skills to magnifying our ability to fully live out our purpose by making a difference through our work.

The process of becoming the best at what we do and being known for what only we can offer begins. It is now legacy in the making because we now focus on our life's work.

Financially, things are okay. We can take care of what we need and maybe a little extra.

Emotionally, we are the most grounded and balanced we've ever been (hopefully).

Spiritually speaking, we continue to grow, and it's part of who we are.

■ Stage Six: Focusing on the one thing.

We know our purpose and our calling.

We choose and strive to streamline all aspect of our lives so it perfectly aligns with our top priorities. We also get to say "no" to what doesn't serve our new way of life and top priorities.

Now it's the time to remind ourselves that we are living our purpose through the vehicle of our calling that we have now defined.

It's important at this stage to find contentment, joy, and peace in knowing just that.

It's also important, in occasional moments of uncertainty, to revisit the signpost you've driven by up to now so you can either know that all is aligned or determine that you need to course-correct. Think of it as a life alignment.

Now. Will there be more challenges and frustrations at this stage? Of course there will be.

A big one at this stage can be related to our financial situation. Because of the needed transition into pursuing our calling fully, some sort of financial sacrifice may be required. It can be in the form of earning less money, having a tighter and sometimes painfully tighter budget or having to financially *glide*—as I like to call it—by relying on our savings. It can also be a combination of those different scenarios.

Emotionally speaking, we are as emotionally and spiritually grounded as we've ever been.

Spiritually speaking, we become increasingly aware and allow ourselves to be guided by our heart and our spirit. We are guided in ways that can help us practically create and maintain fulfilling lives on a daily basis. We go through life efficiently at this point by focusing on what truly matters and letting go of the rest.

These different stages I've shared are not perfect representations of what we go through in life. In some cases there could be more stages or less stages. Some items in the stages could be experienced in another stage as well.

The point for doing this is so we can have something tangible that our mind can more easily process and, as a result, find its bearings.

If you have any questions related to what I've just shared with you or this book in general, please let me know. I can't wait to hear from you. Find out how you can share your thoughts and ideas in the resources section at the end of this book.

If there was anything I'd want to leave you with before you finish reading this book is this:

The purpose journey has a spiritual dimension that I suggest not ignoring. As such, follow the spiritual path before anything else when looking for direction and answers, for this is the path that will give you all the answers you seek. Even those you don't know you're looking for and need. But your spirit, your soul, needs them and are looking for them so they—and you—can break free.

Follow that path, and everything else will be given to you. Go down the spiritual rabbit hole, and you'll be sure to find what it is that will feel like home.

Now it's time to come full circle and for you to state what your purpose is and what your calling (vehicle) is in relations to your purpose and, finally, who you feel you're called to help and serve.

Remember that the answer you seek is within you, and you reading this book up to now has prepared you to be able to write your one true answer. So take a moment to go in silent introspection, feel your heart, go inward to get the answer as it relates to the greater purpose.

Go ahead. Let it flow out of you.

My dear friend,

You've made it to the end of this book!

From the very, very, bottom of my heart (you have no idea), I want to thank you for having taken the time out of your busy life to read this book.

I thank you for being open to reading my perspective on this fascinating topic of purpose and allowing me to share a little bit of my life and purpose journey with you. It is a purpose journey that I've been on and studying for over ten years now.

My hope is that, based on the overview that I gave you, the content of this book will serve you time and time again as you revisit and move forward on your own purpose journey.

I want to hear from you, so please be sure to let me know how this book impacted you and your life. Second to the love I experience with my loved ones, nothing is going to bring me more joy than to hear your story of transformation and fulfillment. Email me and connect with me on my blog.

Again, I'm here to support you at every stage of this unique and exciting purpose journey, so stay in touch, and let me know how I can be help.

With so much appreciation and gratitude,

Your faithful companion.

Here to help you live your purpose,

Mick.

ACKNOWLEDGEMENTS

Me getting to this point has been quite the journey, and it's important that I mention those whose actions and character have made such a difference in my life.

My deepest gratitude goes to Frank G. Miglorie, former President of the College of St. Joseph, VT, and his wife, Patricia Miglorie, for their generosity, understanding, trust, and support towards me and my family and for making me feel as a member of the College of St. Joseph family. Along with the CSJ team, particularly Jerry Tofferi for his patience and Kristie Johnson, I'm grateful for them making me feel at home when I was away from home. My family and I are forever grateful to you.

A special heartfelt thank you goes to Coach Mark Benetatos, Coach B., for taking me under his wing, his mentorship, believing in me, seeing the potential in me, and showing me what it took to be a winner, a champion, on the basketball court and in life.

To Pr. Lokangaka Losambe and Aunt Bibi for taking care of me while I was away from home and being my parents while living in the U.S. I'm forever grateful.

Of course, the teachers and professors who have contributed to my intellectual growth, open-mindedness, and critical thinking by exposing me to new ideas and different ways of thinking, and challenging me. Their influence has contributed to me being who I am today, and I thank them for that.

To Darryl Humphrey, Kevan Seng, and his family, I'm forever grateful to you for being there when I needed it the most. The world needs more generous, helpful, and thoughtful souls like yours.

To Moctar Diouf for being there through my ups and down, for his friendship, loyalty, and always having my back. Thanks for that, brother.

I want to thank Kenya Kondo and Dominique Dubrule for taking the time out of their busy schedule to read the first draft of this book and for giving me their honest feedback. Their feedback is what has helped this book be a better version of what it would've been had I decided to go at it alone. Speaking of helping this book be the best version that it could be, a huge thank you to the FriesenPress team for their invaluable support and expertise which helped me bring the final version of this book to life.

I also owe a big part of where I am today spiritually—and how I was led to integrate into my life the Peaceful State Process (PSP)—to the man who not only healed me in a miraculous way from what I had been suffering from for about a decade (that's a story for another book) but whose healing led me to be curious about the place God had in my life, how He works, and learn more about this man called Jesus. Brother Robert Canton, from the bottom of my heart, thank you for the unexpected miracle that gave me hope again.

My life growing up has been such an adventure. I have moved from country to country and become what's known to as a Third Culture Kid (TCK). For this rich and adventurous life, my gratitude goes to my dad, a man for whom I have the utmost respect. He is a man who I've grown up to view as the most hard-working, self-sacrificing good man I've ever met. He is full of wisdom and devoted to the well-being of his family. "Papa", thank you for everything.

To my sisters, thank you for always having my back. You are my guardian angels.

Last but not least, I want to thank my mom for her uncondi-
tional love and nurturing. I also want to thank her for trusting
her instincts and bringing me home. She later pointed me in a
direction that would lead me to cross path with Brother Robert
Canton and reconnect with God in the most unexpected way. It is
because of her that I have my life back.

"Maman", I thank God for you and for everything else in my life.

© Darryl Humphrey Photography

Real Life Mechanics.
Live Your Purpose

ABOUT THE AUTHOR

Mick Lolekonda helps people live their purpose.

Specializing on the topic of purpose, Mick studies its application relative to creating the fulfilling lives that we feel we're meant to have and building meaningful businesses, as well as careers, in line with our purpose and calling in life.

Mick is a mentor, a spiritual guide, and an advisor who supports individuals who feel have a purpose and want to get on the path that they feel called to pursue while making a difference with helping people, organizations, and even within their industries. These purpose-driven individuals have included professionals and aspiring entrepreneurs, founders of companies, consultants, and team leaders.

His online show, Real Life Mechanics, where he interviews people who have found their calling, love what they do, and are making a difference, can be watched on his blog.

Each year, Mick is available to speak at conferences, universities, and organizations.

Visit MickLolekonda.com for further information on his mentorship services and programs. You can also contact him for speaking inquiries.

COMPLIMENTARY RESOURCES

- Download complimentary resources there to help you live and stay connected to your true purpose when subscribing to Mick's newsletter at:

www.RealLifeMechanics.com/subscribe.